Masterpieces from Dresden

ROYAL ACADEMY OF ARTS

This edition first published on
the occasion of the exhibition
'Masterpieces from Dresden'

Royal Academy of Arts, London
15 March – 8 June 2003

Sponsored by

EXHIBITION CURATORS
Harald Marx
Norman Rosenthal
Cecilia Treves

EXHIBITION ORGANISATION
Emeline Max
Anne Starkey

PHOTOGRAPHIC AND COPYRIGHT
CO-ORDINATION
Miranda Bennion

CATALOGUE
Royal Academy Publications
David Breuer
Harry Burden
Carola Krueger
Fiona McHardy
Peter Sawbridge
Nick Tite

Translated from the German
by Malcolm Green

Designed by Isambard Thomas
Colour origination by DawkinsColour
Printed in Italy by Graphicom

Copyright © 2003
Royal Academy of Arts, London

BRITISH LIBRARY
CATALOGUING-IN-PUBLICATION DATA
A catalogue record for this book is
available from the British Library

ISBN 1-903973-27-9 (paperback)

ISBN 1-903973-26-0 (hardback)

Distributed outside the United States
and Canada by Thames & Hudson Ltd,
London

Distributed in the United States and
Canada by Harry N. Abrams, Inc.,
New York

EDITOR'S NOTE
Measurements are given in centimetres,
height before width (before depth,
in the case of cat. 12).

All works in this exhibition have
been generously lent by the Staatliche
Kunstsammlungen Dresden,
Gemäldegalerie Alte Meister,
unless otherwise stated.

CATALOGUE CONTRIBUTORS
KB   Kathrin Bürger
JG   Jürgen Gottschalk
AH   Andreas Henning
EH   Elisabeth Hipp
OK   Oliver Kase
SK   Stephan Kemperdick
KK   Karin Kolb
HM   Harald Marx
UN   Uta Neidhardt
MCS Marie Catherine Sahut
MS   Monika Schäfer
GS   Gerd Spitzer
DW   Daniela Weber
GJMW Gregor J. M. Weber
MW   Matthias Weniger
MWo Moritz Woelk

PHOTOGRAPHIC ACKNOWLEDGEMENT
Photos Elke Estel/Hans-Peter Klut
© Staatliche Kunstsammlungen Dresden

ILLUSTRATIONS
Page 2: detail of cat. 35
Pages 6–7: detail of cat. 28
Pages 30–31: detail of cat. 16
Pages 64–65: detail of cat. 32
Pages 110–111: detail of cat. 37
Pages 128–129: detail of cat. 42
Pages 160–161: detail of cat. 57

BERNARDO BELLOTO
DETTO CANALETTO

Forewords

This exhibition comes at an important time for Dresden and its museums. The city has transformed itself since the Second World War and I am delighted to have been asked to contribute to this catalogue.

Last year, Dresden and its surrounding countryside suffered terribly in the wake of torrential rainstorms in which rivers burst their banks and flooded huge swathes of central Europe. Led by Chancellor Gerhard Schröder, the German nation responded magnificently to the plight of the people of Saxony. This exhibition of masterpieces from the Dresden State Art Collections is a signal to us that the city's recovery is now well underway; that her churches, museums and other historic monuments have reopened and are flourishing once again.

I am very happy to join with the German Chancellor in extending to the people of Dresden our support and our thanks for so generously allowing some of their finest works of art to come to London.

The Rt Hon. Tony Blair MP
Prime Minister of Great Britain

The 'Masterpieces from Dresden' exhibition is a further example of the splendid and long-standing co-operation that exists between the Royal Academy of Arts and German museums. Introducing the British public to some of the finest works in the Dresden State Art Collections imbues this co-operation, I believe, with a new and special meaning.

In the first half of the eighteenth century the art-loving Augustus the Strong, Elector of Saxony, and his son Augustus III assembled one of the most outstanding European art collections. Convinced that art is by nature international, they brought to Dresden works of the highest quality from all over Europe. The Italian, Netherlandish, French, Spanish and German masters now on show in London represent a small yet exquisite cross-section of this collection.

Last August it was only by a hair's breadth that the Dresden art collections escaped catastrophe. But for the tireless efforts of countless volunteers, the depots would have been swamped by the devastating floods along the Elbe and thousands of works of art destroyed. In those difficult days the BBC was the first foreign broadcaster to tell the story to the outside world. Help, sympathy and offers of assistance poured in – also and in particular from Britain. Support came from all over the world, support that was profoundly appreciated by people in Dresden, Saxony and throughout Germany.

It was a miracle, too, that Dresden's art collections survived unscathed the bombing of the city in 1945. The message of those events and what led up to them, as we look back today, is that these works are a European heritage which we have an obligation to preserve and safeguard. This exhibition here in London makes an important contribution to that.

I hope the exhibition will attract a great many visitors and would be very pleased if it encourages as many as possible to come and see Dresden and its artistic heritage for themselves.

Gerhard Schröder
Chancellor of the Federal Republic of Germany

It will be very exciting for me to see posters of paintings from the Dresden collections in the London tube. I hope that they will also act as an advertisement for Dresden itself. Saxony has a long tradition as a state and as a cultural centre. During the eighteenth century, the region reached the peak of its ascendancy under Augustus the Strong. Dresden's famous cityscape – the Frauenkirche, the Hofkirche and the Palais Brühl – was brought to completion at this period and captured in paint by Bernardo Bellotto.

Although work on the Frauenkirche, which was destroyed during the war, will be complete in 2005, Dresden will never be able to hide all the losses inflicted on its beautiful Baroque architecture by the bombing. Nevertheless, many first-time visitors are surprised to see that many major buildings survived. It goes without saying that Dresden, with its churches, synagogue, theatre and opera house, belongs to the select circle of Europe's leading cultural cities. But above all it is the State Art Collections that draw visitors to Saxony and Dresden. In 2001, some 1.7 million people visited the art collections in the Zwinger Palace, also home to the city's collections of Meissen porcelain, of scientific instruments, and of arms and armour.

During the last twelve months Dresden has endured a major setback. Terrible floods wreaked havoc last August. Dresden's central station and entire districts of the city suffered. Water entered the courtyard of the famous Zwinger and the underground stores of the Gemäldegalerie Alte Meister. Museum staff, with helpers from the ministries, managed to evacuate the paintings in the nick of time by wading through the water without even the help of electric light. Just under three months later, on 9 November, we reopened the Gemäldegalerie Alte Meister, the Semper Opera House and the State Theatre. Although the effects of the flood have yet to be completely overcome, a great deal has already been achieved. We have received help from outside the city, and we are deeply grateful for this solidarity. With the help of friends both at home and abroad, we hope to come up with a good solution for the future.

Professor Georg Milbradt
Minister and President of the State of Saxony

Despite the difficulties caused by the floods of August 2002, the catastrophe has opened up new possibilities for us. We will strive in future towards greater international co-operation, for the Dresden collections are part of the world's cultural heritage. At present their importance stands in marked contrast to the cultural policies we encounter in our day-to-day work.

The fact that we are now able to present this exhibition at the Royal Academy is an indirect result of the floods. Dresden's world-famous collection presents itself for the first time in London with 57 outstanding works. Inevitably this is a small selection, but it is to be hoped that it will tempt visitors to travel to Dresden and experience the wealth and richness of the collection in full.

Although an unparalleled rescue operation on 13–14 August 2002 succeeded in saving all the art works, we are still faced with a difficult situation. Our ultra-modern, underground store for Old Master paintings is unusable. Likewise the storage facilities in the old Renaissance cellars of the Albertinum, home to the Galerie Neue Meister and the Sculpture Collection, have had to be abandoned. Although all our museums have reopened, a number of their exhibition rooms continue to be used as stopgap storage space. We now require a modern and secure storage building in which works of sculpture and paintings can be safeguarded for the future. Planning is underway, but money is short. In order to realise this project, we require political backing in Germany and the support of our friends from around the world. Visitors to this exhibition at the Royal Academy will be helping us: some of the proceeds from sales of the catalogue will help to pay for this new repository. I thank therefore my collaborators at the Royal Academy of Arts and at the Staatliche Museen zu Berlin, who, together with my colleagues at the Gemäldegalerie Alte Meister, have arranged this wonderful exhibition within the shortest time imaginable.

Dr Martin Roth
General Director, Staatliche Kunstsammlungen Dresden

President's Foreword

It was in September last year that Peter-Klaus Schuster, Director-General of the Staatliche Museen zu Berlin, informed us of his intention to stage an exhibition of outstanding paintings from the legendary Dresden Gemäldegalerie. This event, which was inaugurated last December at the Altes Museum in Berlin by Chancellor Gerhard Schröder, was to take place in the wake of the terrible damage wrought by the River Elbe last summer.

The Staatliche Kunstsammlungen Dresden are notable for their extraordinary richness and diversity. The early eighteenth century saw the foundation of the Green Vault, with its startling *objets d'art*, the Sculpture Collection, the Print Cabinet and Dresden's unique porcelain holdings. These represent only part of the princely collections amassed by the Electors of Saxony, who also acquired an impressive armoury and a unique collection of scientific instruments.

Later purchasing activity formed the basis of today's Galerie Neue Meister with its outstanding nineteenth- and twentieth-century paintings. An astonishing group of works by Caspar David Friedrich and his school forms part of this collection, housed today in the Albertinum. But perhaps the greatest jewel of Dresden's many extraordinary art collections are the outstanding Old Master paintings displayed in the Gemäldegalerie Alte Meister designed by Gottfried Semper.

Contrasting with the Baroque architecture of the Zwinger Palace whose fourth side it forms, Semper's gallery building was completed in 1855. After the destruction of Dresden in 1945 the gallery, which suffered major damage, was painstakingly rebuilt along with many historic monuments, churches and theatres. Today, while the Staatliche Kunstsammlungen Dresden campaign for new safe storage rooms for their treasures, we have

a rare opportunity to show some of their masterpieces. Some of the proceeds from sales of this catalogue will go towards the fund for this new repository.

The Royal Academy wishes to express its sincere thanks to Dr Martin Roth, General Director of the Staatliche Kunstsammlungen Dresden, and to Dr Harald Marx, Dr Ulrich Bischoff and Dr Moritz Woelk, custodians of the collections that have lent so generously to this exhibition. We owe a special debt of gratitude to Dr Marx, Director of the Gemäldegalerie Alte Meister for many years, who has played an instrumental role in bringing about the exhibition and its catalogue. We are deeply grateful to him and to all his colleagues for their scholarship and commitment to this project.

In London we would like to thank His Excellency the German Ambassador Thomas Matussek as well as Tilman Hankel, Cultural Attaché at the German Embassy, for championing this proposal from the outset. Finally, this magnificent exhibition would not have been possible without the generous sponsorship of ABN AMRO, with additional support from private benefactors, including Louise Blouin MacBain, Katrin Bellinger and the Blackstone Group, together with others who wish to remain anonymous.

We feel privileged indeed to be able to present these masterpieces – a mere taste of the glories that Dresden has to offer – in London. Already, only months after the floodwaters have subsided, the Gemäldegalerie Alte Meister with its incomparable paintings has reopened. It is our hope that this exhibition will encourage you to visit the Florence of the Elbe: you will not be disappointed.

Professor Phillip King CBE
President of the Royal Academy of Arts

Sponsor's Preface

ABN AMRO is delighted to sponsor 'Masterpieces from Dresden' at the Royal Academy of Arts, an exhibition that promises to be one of this year's cultural highlights in Europe.

The exhibition comprises a selection of masterpieces ranging from paintings by Mantegna, Canaletto and Titian, to works by Poussin, Rubens and Van Dyck. This selection of paintings was rescued last August from the Zwinger Palace in Dresden when the River Elbe's rising floodwaters rushed through the building's vaults and threatened to destroy one of Europe's greatest art collections. The Royal Academy now has the opportunity to exhibit part of this collection, showing pieces never before seen outside Germany.

At ABN AMRO, we believe it is of the utmost importance to be an active and responsible member of the societies and communities in which we are present. This includes a strong commitment to cultural activities and it is for this reason that we are very pleased to be associated with this exceptional project.

We trust that many people will enjoy this unique exhibition.

Rijkman Groenink
Chairman of the
Managing Board
ABN AMRO Bank

Wilco Jiskoot
Member of the
Managing Board
ABN AMRO Bank

Thoughts and Observations on the Dresden Gemäldegalerie

Harald Marx

'Interspersed with artistic paintings'
THE ELECTORS' KUNSTKAMMER AS THE GERM OF THE LATER COLLECTIONS

'The same lavishness that … went into developing and perfecting Dresden's outward appearance in the eighteenth century also fed, enriched and enlarged that vital part of its inner substance, the treasures of the Arts and Sciences, to which Dresden is indebted – perhaps more so than to its outward charms – for its position as one of Europe's most privileged cities.'[1] As Martin Bernhard Lindau wrote these lines in 1885, he was quite clear in his mind that the Gemäldegalerie held an outstanding place among these treasures.

Although the gallery is very much a creation of the first half of the eighteenth century, Lindau knew that Dresden had been home to important paintings at a much earlier date: as well as his much-cited *Geschichte der königlichen Haupt- und Residenzstadt Dresden* (1885) and his *Dresdener Galeriebuch* (1856),[2] his biography of Lucas Cranach the Elder (1883) gives an exhaustive account of the relations of Cranach the father and Cranach the son with the Albertine line of the Wettins, who resided in Dresden and Freiberg.[3]

Cranach the Elder portrayed Duke George the Bearded, and as early as 1514 Duke Henry the Pious (fig. 1); in 1552 Lucas Cranach the Younger painted three large panels depicting scenes from the life of Hercules for Elector Maurice, which were kept in the Tower Room of the Residenzschloss in Dresden.[4] Two of these have been preserved in the Gemäldegalerie. There were of course many other paintings in the palace, but these works by the Cranachs served a representative or decorative purpose and had a political agenda to fulfil: there was no thought yet of an art collection in the later sense.

Likewise paintings played only a subordinate role in the Electoral Kunstkammer, or chamber of art, in Dresden. This was founded by Elector Augustus (1526–1586) and inaugurated in 1560, the year in which the first inventory was compiled.[5] This universal collection, which contained objects culled from every conceivable field of knowledge and was thus a picture of the known world at that time, reflected the claim to power made by the Renaissance prince who owned it and could arrange its contents systematically in his cabinet.

The Elector Augustus's Kunstkammer was one of numerous cabinets created north of the Alps during the second half of the sixteenth century as a result of the rise of Humanism during the Renaissance. Old inventories and even printed lists and descriptions of cabinets from the seventeenth and eighteenth centuries reveal that paintings were very much a secondary matter. In 1671 Tobias Beutel, for instance, describes the 'first cabinet', which contained above all 'mathematical

Fig. 1
Lucas Cranach the Elder,
Duke Henry the Pious, 1514.
Oil on panel transferred to
canvas, 184 × 82.5 cm.

Staatliche Kunstsammlungen
Dresden, Gemäldegalerie Alte
Meister, Gal. no. 1906 G

OPPOSITE
Detail of fig. 18

implements … Likewise yet another writing desk / with mathematical instruments, and additionally many cases full of mechanical tools. A long board for games / and on the walls above this / Biblical paintings / in Lucas Kranach's hand / and other artistic painters.' The 'Third cabinet. Caskettes and art paintings' contained a sizeable number of works attributed to artists of high standing. Beutel remarked: 'Finally this cabinet is, like all the others, interspersed with artistic paintings old and new, painted for example by Albrecht Dürer, Luca von Leyden, Luca Cranach, by Tintoretto, Titiano, Rubens, as well as by other artistic painters.'[6]

'His Roy. Majesty's Picture Cabinets'
THE PICTURE COLLECTION UNDER KING AUGUSTUS THE STRONG

A new era dawned for the arts and collecting with the reign of Elector Frederick Augustus I (1670–1733), who from 1697 was also King of Poland and as such was known as Augustus II.[7] His exceptional physical powers earned him the popular epithet Augustus the Strong. He followed the example of his fellow German princes and began to collect *objets d'art* and paintings, soon outstripping his royal colleagues.[8] Augustus the Strong had paintings purchased in Italy and above all in the Netherlands and Flanders, not only individual pieces but sometimes entire collections. His First Court Painter and Superintendent of Paintings, Samuel Bottschild, played an important role in this. This period saw the arrival of the *Sleeping Venus* by Giorgione and Titian (fig. 2) in 1699, and in 1709 Rubens's *Diana Returning from the Hunt* (cat. 43).

But Augustus the Strong's most important adviser in art matters was Raymond Leplat, whose title from 1698, 'Ordonneur du Cabinet', did scant justice to his importance. Over a period of thirty years he acquired numerous paintings, sculptures and pieces of furniture for Augustus, either personally or through agents in Paris, Antwerp and Italy. Leplat was also the creator of the Dresden sculpture collection.[9] Two further advisers and mediators should be named alongside Leplat: the influential cabinet minister Count Jacob Heinrich von Flemming, and Field Marshal Count Christoph August von Wackerbarth, Director of Public Buildings. Wackerbarth, a collector himself, played an especially decisive part in building up the Gemäldegalerie during those years, and brought a particularly large number

Fig. 2
Giorgione, *Sleeping Venus*, c. 1508–10. Oil on canvas, 108.5 × 175 cm.

Staatliche Kunstsammlungen Dresden, Gemäldegalerie Alte Meister, Gal. no. 185

of Netherlandish pieces to Dresden. Lorenzo Rossi, who was appointed Court Painter in 1721, acted as an art agent in Italy, and was responsible for the arrival of Palma Vecchio's *Venus* (fig. 3) in Saxony from Venice in 1728.

There was no space in the Kunstkammer for all these acquisitions, and nor were they intended for such a location. Instead, they were integrated into the state rooms of the Residenzschloss, in which they were soon housed in their own gallery where they could be displayed on a wall facing the windows. On 28 February 1707 the Superintendent of the Kunstkammer, Tobias Beutel, and the Superintendent of Paintings, Heinrich Christoph Fehling, completed and signed their 'Specification of those paintings that his Royal Majesty and Electoral Highness of Saxony most kindly wishes to have removed from His Kunstkammer...and to be brought and hung in the Ball Room, as well as in other rooms.' The list, which has not survived, consisted of 614 paintings.[10] At that stage Augustus the Strong still believed that the paintings and sculptures should be presented together, so in 1712 he charged Leplat with bringing 28 bronzes from the Kunstkammer in order to have them displayed 'in His Roy. Majesty's Picture Cabinets'.[11] Augustus the Strong was also to insist in his later museum projects that marble statues, busts and bronze sculptures be displayed in the gallery rooms (cat. 12). The ground plan, for instance, of the second storey of the Residenzschloss in Dresden, which was engraved in 1719 on the occasion of the marriage of the electoral heir, Augustus III, later King of Poland, to the Austrian Archduchess Maria Josepha, the daughter of Emperor Joseph I, shows a 'grande gallerie des Tableaux Statue Et buste de marbre groupes Et Statue de bronze'.[12]

From 1722 to 1728 the King's Privy Chamberlain, Adam Friedrich Steinhäuser, drew up a separate inventory of paintings at the Residenzschloss in Dresden and the castles of Pillnitz and Moritzburg, as well as those kept at several other locations. The designation 'gallery and adjoining rooms' in the inventory refers to the above-mentioned rooms in the Residenzschloss.

Shortly afterwards, the paintings were moved to the Riesensaal (Great Hall), which had been specially converted for the purpose, even if its furnishings were always to remain somewhat temporary. The windows onto the courtyard were boarded up with planks to create a tall, continuous wall on which to hang the works. Johann George Keyssler visited Dresden in 1730 and subsequently described the picture gallery in his travel journal. He describes the Riesensaal, which also

Fig. 3
Palma Vecchio, *Venus*, *c.* 1520. Oil on canvas, 112.5 × 186 cm.

Staatliche Kunstsammlungen Dresden, Gemäldegalerie Alte Meister, Gal. no. 190

Fig. 4
Hans Holbein the Younger,
*Portrait of Charles de Solier,
Sieur de Morette*, 1534/35.
Oil on oak panel,
92.5 × 75.5 cm.

Staatliche Kunstsammlungen
Dresden, Gemäldegalerie Alte
Meister, Gal. no. 1890

contained sculptures and vases of porphyry and serpentine, as well as the adjoining rooms that were dedicated individually to portraits, fruit and flower pieces, and landscapes. Keyssler also noted that: 'The old, famous paintings by Holbein, Cranach etc. are to be found together in two rooms.'[13]

Augustus the Strong was fully aware of the provisional character of this 'gallery', and his museum plans after 1730 foresaw a picture gallery situated at the end of the Zwinger and its pavilions and galleries, which had received a new function since 1728 as the 'Palais Royal des Sciences'.[14] A new epoch in both collecting and displaying the paintings was not, however, to be witnessed in Dresden until the reign of Augustus's son, King Augustus III.

'My amazement surpassed every expectation'
THE GEMÄLDEGALERIE AS THE CREATION
OF KING AUGUSTUS III

The death of Augustus the Strong in 1733 and the assumption of power by his son did not result in an immediate change in course for the arts and collecting in Dresden, but with time an appreciable modification in the tastes and interests evinced in acquisitions took place. Like his father, the new king was a person with a profound attachment to the arts, and likewise an authority in many fields. The 'Kavaliersreise', the German equivalent of the Grand Tour, that he undertook between 1711 and 1719 around Europe, especially to France and Italy, had taught him much.

It is easy to understand why art and court life came to assume such a multinational character during Augustus III's reign, given his biography. His father, Augustus the Strong, was compelled to adopt the Catholic faith in 1697 in order to become King of Poland. The Elector and later King Augustus III converted to Catholicism in 1712 while in Bologna during his Kavaliersreise, at first keeping it

Fig. 5
Jan van Eyck, *Winged
Altarpiece*, 1437.
Oil on oak panel:
central panel 33.1 × 27.5 cm;
side panels each 33.1 ×
13.6 cm.

Staatliche Kunstsammlungen
Dresden, Gemäldegalerie Alte
Meister, Gal. no. 799

secret.[15] His conversion led to a strengthening of Catholicism in Dresden that was not to be without its influence on the collection, although artistic quality and not subject matter seems always to have been the ultimate criterion for the purchase of a painting.

Under Augustus III's reign, the collection reached its zenith, and resulted in what we now know and admire as the Dresdener Gemäldegalerie. Little of this was to be sensed in the 1730s, but from around 1740 a great deal of work and commitment, and at times every available penny, went into expanding the collection. It was during this time that Dresden's holdings achieved their great reputation in Europe. Acquisitions continued to be made until the outbreak of the Seven Years War in 1756, at which point they halted, never again to be repeated on the same scale.

We see from this that the Dresden Gemäldegalerie came into being over a period of about fifty years, with works being acquired not by scholars but by two rulers who were connoisseurs and lovers of the arts, and who represented the best of court taste at their time. They were responsible for the strengths and weaknesses of the collection, indeed for its very character: masterpieces of the High Renaissance and Baroque from Italy; primarily seventeenth-century paintings from the Netherlands; and numerous paintings of outstanding quality by the so-called 'Little Dutch Masters', such as the exquisite group by the Leiden Feinmaler.[16] Seventeenth-century masterpieces from France, such as works by Nicolas Poussin and Claude Lorrain (cats 36, 37), were also included. Dürer, Cranach and Holbein were likewise collected as the leading representatives of German art; some examples, indeed, were already to be found in the Kunstkammer. At times, however, attributions were confused. Jan van Eyck's small *Winged Altarpiece* (fig. 5) was attributed to Dürer, and Holbein's *Sieur de Morette* (fig. 4) regarded as a work by Leonardo da Vinci. By and large, early Italian paintings and Spanish art in general were absent, and only came to be collected in the mid- to late nineteenth century.

Fig. 6
Rembrandt, *Ganymede*, 1635.
Oil on canvas, 177 × 130 cm.

Staatliche Kunstsammlungen
Dresden, Gemäldegalerie Alte
Meister, Gal. no. 1558

Fig. 7
Correggio, *The Holy Night*,
1522–30. Oil on poplar panel,
256 × 188 cm

Staatliche Kunstsammlungen
Dresden, Gemäldegalerie Alte
Meister, Gal. no. 152

Fig. 8
Titian, *The Tribute Money*,
c. 1516. Oil on poplar panel,
75 × 56 cm.

Staatliche Kunstsammlungen
Dresden, Gemäldegalerie Alte
Meister, Gal. no. 169

Fig. 9
Andrea del Sarto, *The Sacrifice of Abraham*, *c.* 1527/28. Oil on poplar panel, 213 × 159 cm.

Staatliche Kunstsammlungen Dresden, Gemäldegalerie Alte Meister, Gal. no. 77

Fig. 10
Jan Vermeer, *The Procuress*, 1656. Oil on canvas, 143 × 130 cm.

Staatliche Kunstsammlungen Dresden, Gemäldegalerie Alte Meister, Gal. no. 1335

During the eighteenth century, paintings streamed into Dresden from all over Europe: from Italy,[17] Paris,[18] Amsterdam, Prague and Vienna. Acquisitions were supervised by the Prime Minister, Count Heinrich von Brühl, and Carl Heinrich von Heineken, Brühl's secretary and from 1746 Director of the Royal Print Collection. Brühl and Heineken enlisted the help not only of artists and dealers as their agents, but even of ministers and diplomats. Heineken was also directly instrumental in acquiring among other works Elsheimer's *Jupiter and Mercury at the House of Philemon and Baucis* (cat. 10), as well as the *Ganymede* by Rembrandt (fig. 6).

It is of course impossible to discuss the era of King Augustus III without mentioning his Prime Minister, who from 1738 was the most powerful man at court. Brühl held the reins in both politics as well as questions of art, always acting in his own interests as well as to uphold the glory of his monarch. He had an extremely important art collection himself, which came to include around one thousand paintings. In 1744 this was given its own gallery on the so-called Brühlsche Terrasse in Dresden.[19]

But all royal acquisitions were eclipsed in 1745 by the purchase of the hundred best paintings from the collection of Francesco III, Duke of Modena.[20] These consisted of major works of the Italian Renaissance, and were quite unlike anything owned by collectors north of the Alps at that time. Among them were four large altarpieces by Correggio (fig. 7);[21] Titian's *The Tribute Money* (fig. 8); the four large paintings by Veronese that had been painted for the Cuccina family; the Ferrarese paintings brought to Modena after the Este family had been ousted from Ferrara, including magnificent works by Garofalo, Dosso and Battista Dossi, and even by Gerolamo da Carpi;[22] the *Sacrifice of Abraham* by Andrea del Sarto (fig. 9); several works that take us into the seventeenth century or that already belong to the Baroque by Annibale Carracci, Guido Reni and Guercino; and, moreover, paintings by Velázquez, Rubens and Holbein.[23]

At a stroke, this purchase elevated a notable royal yet provincial holding into a collection of European standing. And the buying went on, again in Italy. From 1746 it was supervised by the newly appointed Gallery Superintendent Pietro Maria Guarienti, who also compiled an inventory of the Dresden collection. By 1742, following the death of Raymond Leplat, Johann Gottfried Riedel had also become a Superintendent. Riedel was a painter, a restorer and an authority on paintings. In 1741, he had arranged a major purchase in Vienna, and in the same year he managed to acquire 268 pictures from the Wallenstein Collection in Dux (Bohemia): these included *The Procuress* by Jan Vermeer (fig. 10) and two small portraits by Frans Hals. More works followed in 1748, this time 69 paintings from the Imperial Collection in Prague, including Rubens's *Wild Boar Hunt* (fig. 11).

The culmination of this expansion was the acquisition of the *Sistine Madonna* (fig. 12) in 1754, a work that came from the monastery church of San Sisto in Piacenza, for 20,000 ducats. With that, a long-cherished wish of King Augustus III, the ownership of an undisputed masterpiece by Raphael, was at last fulfilled.

The upshot of all these purchases was that sweeping changes had to be made in order to accommodate them. Until this point the gallery collection itself and works by the Dresden court painters had been kept in the Residenzschloss. In the *Neues Europäisches Historisches Reise-Lexicon*, edited by Carl Christian Schramm and published in 1744, we read: 'The most excellent embellishments are to be admired in the royal ceremonial and audience rooms, among them … marvellous paintings

Fig. 11
Peter Paul Rubens,
The Wild Boar Hunt,
c. 1615/20. Oil on canvas,
136 × 184 cm.

Staatliche Kunstsammlungen
Dresden, Gemäldegalerie Alte
Meister, Gal. no. 962

Fig. 12
Raphael, *The Sistine Madonna*, 1512/13.
Oil on canvas,
269.5 × 201 cm.

Staatliche Kunstsammlungen
Dresden, Gemäldegalerie Alte
Meister, Gal. no. 93

from the greatest artists and from the skilful hand of His Majesty's First Court
Painter, Herr Louis de Sylvestre … together with the nicely arranged Picture Gallery,
which is a precious collection of the most perfect masterpieces of painting, large
and small, and is not to be overlooked.'[24] From 1745 a major conversion of the
Elector's stables on Jüdenhof turned them into a gallery. Master builder was Johann
Christoph Knöffel, who was also responsible for the design. All that he retained
of the original building, which dated from the reign of Elector Christian I, was the
massive vaulted ground floor, with its two side entrances and the double staircase
that had been installed during structural changes carried out in 1730. The two
upper storeys, which had contained elegant suites for guests and from around 1740
had also housed a good number of paintings, were removed. They were replaced
by a tall gallery with arched windows, as can be seen in the painting and etching
by Bellotto from 1749, which also features King Augustus III in the foreground
in his six-horse coach (fig. 14).

In the preface to his two-volume collection of engravings, published in 1753
and 1757, Carl Heinrich von Heineken provided an overview of the new gallery:

'This is a large, rectangular building of considerable size, containing one continuous gallery that doubles back, as it were, so as to divide the building along its length and produce an inner and an outer gallery.'[25] The 'inner' gallery, reserved for Italian painting, bordered the enclosed courtyard, while the windows facing the outside belonged to the 'outer' gallery, which housed all the non-Italian works. The vestibule greeted the visitor with portraits of the collection's founders by Louis de Silvestre, and other French paintings. The original idea of dividing the great width of the building with a central partition wall, thereby creating one row of rooms facing onto the courtyard and a separate outer suite, resulted in an inestimable conservational benefit: very few paintings hung on outside walls, but instead on both sides of the climatically optimal dividing wall (fig. 13).

Descriptions of individual rooms and their furnishings are rare in the older literature. One of the few informative passages is to be found in the second volume of Johann Christian Hasche's *Umständliche Beschreibung Dresdens* (1781–83): 'The ceiling has been left white and unpainted, the walls have been covered in green damask with gold skirtings and matching foliage at the top, and the paintings hang in magnificent sculpted frames.'[26]

The impression of dignity and splendour that the gallery made on its visitors was noted by Johann Wolfgang von Goethe on his first visit in 1768: 'My amazement surpassed every expectation I came with. This room turning back in on itself, reigned over by a magnificence and order amidst perfect silence, the dazzling frames, which had hardly changed since the day they had been gilded, the polished floors, the rooms visited by more viewers than people who came to work – all this produced a unique feeling of solemn splendour that is more akin to the sensation one has upon entering a church, particularly since the adornments of certain temples, and certain objects of devotion, seemed to be displayed here solely for the holy purpose of art.'[27]

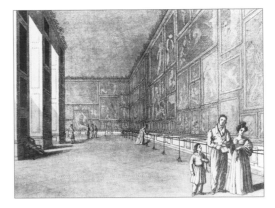

Fig. 13
The dense hang in the 'inner' gallery, lit by large arched windows, 1830. Aquatint.

Staatliche Kunstsammlungen Dresden, Kupferstich-Kabinett

Fig. 14
Bernardo Bellotto.
The Neumarkt in Dresden from the Jüdenhof, 1749.
Oil on canvas, 136 × 237 cm.

Staatliche Kunstsammlungen Dresden, Gemäldegalerie Alte Meister, Gal. no. 610

'A gentleman of standing has an art collection'
ARTISTS, COLLECTORS AND PATRONS

Dresden around the middle of the eighteenth century conjures up for us the names of Augustus III and Count Brühl, images of the royal art collection and the no-less famous opera house, as well as a host of court painters and architects from Italy, France and Germany. But rarely do we remember that a number of private collectors, art lovers and patrons were active at that time in Dresden.[28]

Among those who deserve mention is the minister and learned historian Count Heinrich von Bünau (1697–1762), who employed Johann Joachim Winckelmann (1717–1768) as his librarian from 1748 to 1754 in Nöthnitz.[29] While there Winckelmann befriended the painter Adam Friedrich Oeser (1717–1799), who also worked for Bünau and was later to play an influential role in the arts in Leipzig as Director of the Academy. It was through Oeser that Winckelmann gained an appreciation of the art of his time.

Likewise Carl Heinrich von Heineken, one of the greatest and most erudite authorities on art in his day, owned a collection that ranged from old German masters to works by his contemporaries. In all likelihood painters would have donated works to Heineken's collection, for it was vital to be in his favour if one was to have success with the Prime Minister, and thus at court.[30] Heineken appears to have exploited this situation, and Christian Ludwig von Hagedorn (1713–1780), a diplomat, art theorist and later General Director of the Dresdener Kunstakademie and of the electoral collections in Dresden, complained in 1750 in a letter to his brother, the poet Friedrich von Hagedorn (1708–1754), that he had been coerced into handing over paintings from his own collection to Heineken.[31] In 1756 Heineken auctioned off at least part of his collection through Pierre Remy in Paris.[32]

By the 1740s Hagedorn owned some 200 paintings, mostly contemporary works. A friend of such painters as Johann Alexander Thiele (1685–1752) and Ádám Mányocki (1673–1757), he also knew and esteemed artists such as Franz Christoph Janneck (1703–1761) and Josef Orient (1677–1747) in Vienna. We have precise details of his 'Kabinett', as he called it, for in July 1748 he sent a number of letters to his brother ostensibly addressing various aspects of art in general but in fact written with the chief purpose of lauding his own collection. His aim was to make a good sale of his Kabinett as a whole, but he was never to achieve this. His letters, published in 1797 almost twenty years after his death, and his book *Lettre à un amateur de la peinture*, published in 1755, have provided us with a wealth of information on the lives and doings of the painters and collectors he was close to, information that otherwise would have been lost.[33] The none-too-wealthy Hagedorn reveals a noticeable touch of envy of those who did not have to struggle as he did to live a life with art: 'A gentlemen of standing has an art collection, or as befits his rank a gallery, although there is a difference between the two; he commissions masters of the present day to paint for him, and then decorates whole rooms with those persons' works: this is a most virtuous thing, and the gentleman is referred to as a patron. The Russian ambassador, Count Keyserling, had a whole collection, and his adviser was the painter Dietrich. Naturally he also had the man paint for him. Which led to a whole room being filled with his works, so it could be said that Count Keyserling has an entire collection just of works by Dietrich.'[34] Hagedorn contrasts this with some words in praise of his own collection: 'I could fill three special collections with my paintings by Orient, Brand and Querfurt!, and likewise two special rooms with my works by Mányocki and Nogari![35] Although I am not a distinguished sir, as soon as fortune provides me with the five rooms for this as well as the rooms I need for my other paintings, not forgetting all the necessary furnishings, I too would be above passing judgement on others in these matters.'[36]

This sideswipe is directed at Hermann Karl von Keyserling (1695–1764), whom music-lovers will know as the friend and sponsor of Johann Sebastian Bach, who repaid Keyserling in 1742 by composing the *Goldberg Variations* for him.

Keyserling, a patron of the arts, a friend to artists, a music-lover and a passionate book-collector, was able to combine his cultural ambitions with a successful career as a diplomat. It would be hard to overestimate the part he played in the intricate web of politics, power and culture that linked the courts of St Petersburg, Warsaw, Dresden and Vienna. And wherever he stayed Keyserling gave active support to artists, scholars and musicians. His life perfectly illustrates how multifaceted the artistic world was in the Saxon capital during the years leading up to the Seven Years War (1756–63). In 1741, Keyserling presented Augustus III with a total of over 178 paintings. We do not know what price he received, nor the specific circumstances behind the sale, but in the year of the transaction he was made a Count of the Holy Roman Empire, an honour for which he was surely indebted to Augustus III, who had become Reichsvikar (Regent) of the Empire after the death of Charles VI in 1740. Were the paintings part of a deal? Or an expression of gratitude from the erstwhile baron now raised to count?

If one examines the list of paintings in the Dresden inventory 'prior to 1741' (also known as Steinhäuser's Inventory in 8°) and the sequence of the numbers they were given, it is possible to determine not only connections with certain artists, but also various interrelationships that existed between the Dresden painters themselves. Keyserling owned a magnificent self-portrait by Ismael Mengs, which now resides in the Gemäldegalerie.[37] Keyersling and Mengs knew one another, for the two were music-lovers; indeed, the fact that Anton Raphael Mengs portrayed the singer Domenico Annibali can be explained by Keyserling's close contact with the elder Mengs through their mutual love of music. Similarly Dietrich, Count Keyserling's art adviser, was held in high esteem by both Mengs and Winckelmann, and must have played a role in these circles of artists and musicians. The home of the First Court Painter and Director of the Dresdener Kunstakademie, Louis de Silvestre (cat. 40), was renowned for its music, and it is said that one of his daughters sang in Italian; artists, ministers and foreign ambassadors gathered at Silvestre's home for musical evenings, and doubtless Keyserling was among them.

Just what tight bonds music could form between people of otherwise quite differing character can be seen from a description we have from Gian Lodovico Bianconi (1717–1781), private physician to the heir to the Saxon throne, Frederick Christian (1722–1763), and simultaneously a remarkable writer and authority on art. In his *Historische Lobschrift auf den Ritter Anton Raphael Mengs* Bianconi tells us: 'One evening at Silvestre's house, where Ismael [Mengs] was also present, Annibali sang a moving aria that gained him the applause of all. There are certain arias designed to pluck at the very strings of sensitive hearts, and which are quite irresistible! This one touched Ismael's heart with all it might… O! All-mighty power of music! Ismael is a gruff person, but from that moment on he was unable to resist Annibali, who like an Orpheus began to direct this Norwegian Rhadamanthus as he willed.'[38]

This digression into the world of private collectors and the friendships between artists makes a number of connections clear. We learn that Ismael Mengs was held in esteem by Count Keyserling, who took the advice of Christian Wilhelm Ernst Dietrich in matters of art. People gathered at the house of among others Louis de Silvestre and played music, as was also the case at Keyserling's. Like his teacher, Johann Alexander Thiele, Dietrich was sponsored by Brühl. Similarly, Silvestre was closely connected to the court and above all to Brühl. Christian Ludwig von Hagedorn, who was to play an influential role in Dresden's artistic life after the Seven Years War, collected paintings by Thiele[39] and Dietrich. An important conclusion in all of this is that musicians, visual artists and patrons met on a friendly basis in private; that music was not merely played at court, in the churches and at the opera, but that 'Augustan' Dresden enjoyed fruitful artistic activity on many levels; and that private circles had very distinct points of contact with life at court. This was the artistic and intellectual climate in which the Gemäldegalerie came into being in Dresden.

'In the interest of promoting good taste'
THE GALLERY IN THE SECOND HALF OF THE EIGHTEENTH CENTURY

Just as we can identify tendencies during the era of Augustus the Strong that indicate the growing influence of the young heir and his wife Maria Josepha, the period under Augustus III also shows developments that first resulted in changes after 1763. In political terms these endeavours, prepared and fostered by Augustus III's heir, Frederick Christian,[40] amounted in the widest sense to 're-establishment', and in artistic terms to the championing of bourgeois values. Resistance to Brühl and his profligate methods of government, which had already earned him disapproval by that time, had begun to form during the Seven Years War, even at court. Frederick Christian and his wife, the Bavarian Princess Maria Antonia (1724–1780), became the centre of a silent opposition that extended to all areas of life and the arts.

An appreciable number of artists managed to keep up their reputations not only with the King and Brühl, but also with the future Elector and his wife. Mengs and Dietrich are good examples of this. With time, Johann Joachim Winckelmann sided increasingly with Frederick Christian. Had Frederick Christian ruled longer than three months, Winckelmann might have achieved a number of changes in the Dresden art scene; as Schlechte observed, 'Unlike his father, Augustus III, the heir was not a collector and connoisseur of Italian and Netherlandish art from the period beginning with the Renaissance, but was more interested in researching and reviving Antiquity.'[41] Winckelmann, a friend of Anton Raphael Mengs, said: 'The sole possibility for us to achieve greatness, yes, if possible to become inimitable, is by imitating the ancients.'[42] This was not simply a demand for a change in style: a whole new era was dawning.

Although the second half of the eighteenth century was a quiet time for the Gemäldegalerie as regards new acquisitions, its fame continued to grow. The collection proved important in the development of many Classical and Romantic artists and poets. Eighteenth-century commentators as well as current estimates hail the Gemäldegalerie in Dresden as one of the most important cultural achievements of the 'Augustan' epoch in Saxony.

'Nothing befits a ruler more than choosing his diversions such that the general public will be able to draw pleasant profit from them...It would not be erroneous to term a gallery a place of public learning (école publique), because it is possible to learn under one roof and with but a glance things that otherwise must be sought in a great many books.'[43] This 'enlightened' quotation dates, perhaps surprisingly, from as early as 1753, and comes moreover from Carl Heinrich von Heineken, Count Brühl's secretary. Brühl's role as Prime Minister to King Augustus III is generally given a negative assessment, yet at almost the same time Winckelmann found similar words for the Dresden Gemäldesammlung, and the co-existence of the two quotations strengthens their credibility: 'It is an eternal monument to the magnanimity of our monarch, Augustus III, that in the interest of promoting good taste, the greatest treasures from Italy and the most perfect paintings produced in other lands have been placed here for all the world to view.'[44] Winckelmann alludes here to the installation of the gallery in 1745–47 in the former stables on Jüdenhof. But it was only once the works were hung in their new, purpose-built home that the collection could open its doors and create a sensation; only thus that its wide influence could radiate out over the ensuing decades.

'The new royal museum'
THE GALLERY IN THE NINETEENTH CENTURY

The nineteenth century was to see both gradual changes and decisive breaks. Gallery decisions increasingly became public issues: the appointment of the

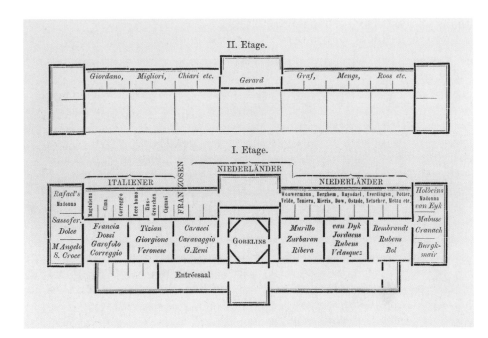

II. Etage.

| Giordano, | Migliori, | Chiari etc. | Gerard | Graf, | Mengs, | Roos etc. |

I. Etage.

NIEDERLÄNDER

ITALIENER | FRANZOSEN | NIEDERLÄNDER

Rafael's Madonna	Maddalena	Cima	Correggio	Ecce homo	Zins-Groschen	Cignani		Houwermann, Berghem, Ruysdael, Everdingen, Potter, Velde, Teniers, Mieris, Dow, Ostade, Netscher, Metzu etc.		Holbeins Madonna von Eyk
Sassofer. Dolce									Mabuse Cranach
M Angelo S. Croce	Francia Dossi Garofolo Correggio	Tizian Giorgione Veronese	Caracci Caravaggio G. Reni	GOBELINS	Murillo Zurbaran Ribera	van Dyk Jordaens Rubens Velasquez	Rembrandt Rubens Bol	Burgkmair

Entréesaal

Fig. 15
The floorplan of the Semperbau, showing the arrangement of paintings by school. From the *Dresdener Galeriebuch*, 1856

Fig. 16
Antonello da Messina, *St Sebastian*, 1475/76. Oil on panel transferred to canvas, 171 × 85.5 cm.

Staatliche Kunstsammlungen Dresden, Gemäldegalerie Alte Meister, Gal. no. 52

'Gallery Commission' in 1836 was a first step in that direction, and the resolution to construct a new building that would meet all the demands of the new century was one notable result, even if the King seemed keener on the idea than the parsimonious representatives of his estates. After much discussion the 'Neue Königliche Museum' was built on the Zwinger. 'Right from the start, the highly imaginative architect Professor Gottfried Semper was chosen to create the design. Semper came up with seven designs complete with models, which were presented on 21 December 1846 before the committee, which was assisted by a number of architects who had been brought in as external experts,' as Wilhelm Schäfer noted in 1860.[45]

The history of the collection is inseparable from its buildings. The architectural demands the pictures made and the way they were hung led to many changes of idea and opinion. But it remained clear that the paintings were to be arranged in a cohesive way according to national and local schools, or in connection with a master, as far as the structure of the buildings permitted (fig. 15).

The middle of the nineteenth century saw a renewed if gradual increase in acquisitions. Although these were now chiefly nineteenth-century paintings (at this time the paintings were purchased that were later to form the Galerie Neue Meister), a number of shifts in emphasis can be recognised among the old masters. Fifteen seventeenth-century Spanish paintings, for instance, arrived in Dresden in 1853 from the estate of Louis Philippe of France, the 'Citizen King', who had died in exile in London after being deposed in 1848. They came at a time when little was known in Germany about Spanish art, and it was only with their arrival that a Spanish section was inaugurated in Dresden.[46] In addition, a number of outstanding paintings by Italian and Netherlandish masters found their way into the collection as late as the 1870s and 1880s.

These additions led to a change in the character of the collection, and a decisive one at that. Karl Woermann discusses this in the introduction to his 1887 catalogue: 'In 1873 the regional parliament granted the allocation of an appreciable sum of money for the enlargement of the royal collections, and for the needs incurred by current art; and these finances were employed to buy various Italian paintings for the Gemäldegalerie such as the *St Sebastian* by Antonello da Messina in 1873 [fig. 16], the *Madonna* by Lorenzo di Credi in 1874 [fig. 17] and Mantegna's precious *Holy Family* [cat. 17] in 1876.'[47] In a more general sense it can be said that the remarkable collection of Italian Quattrocento painting first came into being during the

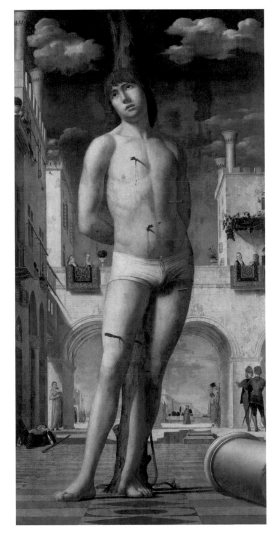

nineteenth century, although some purchases were made prior to the financial injection mentioned by Woermann.

The supervision of the gallery had for many years been in the hands of painters. The Superintendents were Johann Gottfried Riedel (1742–55, with Johann Adam Steinhäuser, who died in 1752); Riedel's son Johann Anton Riedel (1755–1816); Carl Friedrich Demiani (1816–23); Friedrich Matthäi (1823–45);[48] from 1845 to 1871, the Director was Julius Schnorr von Carolsfeld;[49] and from 1871 to 1882 Julius Hübner.[50] From 1882 a new régime began in which art historians held the post, beginning with Karl Woermann. This was an important change, because it allowed a rigorous examination of the collection and its documentation in catalogues. Woermann retired in 1910, to be succeeded by Hans Posse (1910–42) and then Hermann Voss (1942–45).[51]

The main influence of the collection while under the direction of artists, some of whom also taught at the Dresdener Kunstakademie or even acted as its principals (as did Julius Schnorr von Carolsfeld), was on developments in art in Dresden (fig. 18). As early as 1777 Benjamin Gottfried Weinart wrote: 'Even if this Academy [the Dresdener Kunstakademie] has not the strength of numbers as many others have, the electoral Gallery nevertheless provides a wealth of those forms of instruction that such institutions offer…so that pupils who have learnt the

Fig. 17
Lorenzo di Credi, *Madonna with the Christ Child and St John the Baptist.* Oil on poplar panel, 37 × 27 cm.

Staatliche Kunstsammlungen Dresden, Gemäldegalerie Alte Meister, Gal. no. 13

Fig. 18
Karl Louis Preusser, *In the
Dresden Gallery*, 1881. Oil
on canvas, 68 × 87 cm.

Staatliche Kunstsammlungen
Dresden, Galerie Neue Meister,
Inv. no. 94/05

basics can then educate themselves from these wonder-works of art.'[52] Academy and
gallery remained allied in precisely this way throughout the nineteenth century.

A host of young artists came to Dresden for their training, and left with deep
impressions from the works hanging in the Gemäldegalerie. Francesco Casanova[53]
and Konrad Gessner[54] can be named for the eighteenth century, Philipp Otto Runge
for the years around 1800,[55] and for the nineteenth century Alfred Rethel, who in
1842 wrote to his brother after visiting Dresden that the sight of the *Sistine Madonna*
had strengthened his conviction that he was going in the right direction.[56]

'The mirror of man'
THE GALLERY IN THE TWENTIETH CENTURY

Growing demands for a more systematic approach to art history, a looser outlook
on the way paintings should be hung, and a steadily growing collection of 'new'
masters at the beginning of the century made an additional building necessary to
house the 'modern section'. In May 1914, shortly before the outbreak of the First
World War, the Saxon parliament granted the allocation of funds, and in 1916 work
commenced on the building by the Zwingerteich. In a design by Oskar Pusch based
freely on Renaissance forms, it would have made a strong complement to the
buildings on the Theaterplatz, had it been finished. The events of the ensuing
years made any continuation of the work unthinkable, and now not even a trace
remains of this beautiful project, which never developed beyond its foundations.[57]
A relocation of the Galerie Neue Meister was imperative for reasons of space,
however, with the result that its works were first put in the building at 7 Parkstrasse,
before some went to the east hall of the Semperbau, and then in 1931 into the
building of the Sekundogenitur, to be moved after the war to Schloss Pillnitz and
in 1965 to the Albertinum.[58]

Throughout its existence, the Gemäldegalerie had not been immune to political
and economic developments, but its fate seemed sealed as the twentieth century
brought nationwide catastrophe. The era of National Socialism inflicted severe
losses on the modern masters in 1937, when 'decadent' works were confiscated, and
during the Second World War the very existence of the collection was endangered

in a way unparalleled in its entire history. Hans Posse was initially removed from his position as Director in 1933 when the National Socialists assumed power, but was later reinstated and furthermore entrusted with the development of the museum that Adolf Hitler was planning for his home town, Linz.[59]

The Gemäldegalerie had already closed its doors in 1938 before the occupation of Sudetenland, and again in 1939 before the conquest of Poland. Then, when the military offensive and its horrors rebounded on Germany and massive bombing attacks were stepped up in 1942, the paintings were removed to safety. Towards the end of the war, as Russian troops were closing in, the storage facilities east of the Elbe were abandoned in favour of bomb-proof locations to the west of the river, such as the Cottaer Tunnel in the sandstone works at Rottwerndorf, and in the limestone mines of Pockau-Lengefeld.

On 13 February 1945 Dresden was destroyed. Semper's museum building and the Zwinger were seriously damaged. On the entry of the Russian troops into Dresden, 'trophy commissions' were charged with inspecting the works of the Dresden collections and deciding what should be allowed to remain in Germany and what was to be taken away. The central location for bringing together and inspecting the paintings was Schloss Pillnitz, which was undamaged. Consignments of all that was considered valuable were packed there before being shipped to Moscow and Kiev. It looked as though the works would be lost to Dresden for ever.[60]

Activities in the Dresden museums were resumed on a modest scale directly after the war. On 6 July 1946 Schloss Pillnitz opened as a central museum, bringing together all the remnants of Dresden's art collections, left behind more or less by chance, including works from the Gemäldegalerie Alte Meister. An active if provincial period of museum work began, and for about ten years there was no sign of change. But on 25 August 1955 a declaration of the Soviet government was handed over in Moscow to a delegation of the government of the German Democratic Republic stating that Dresden's paintings were to return home.

The paintings were displayed in 1955/56 in two large-scale special exhibitions, first in Moscow, then in Berlin, making them available to the public for the first time in seventeen years. Work on the first leg of the reconstruction of the building (the central section and east wing) was completed on 15 May 1956. The reopening of the Dresdener Gemäldegalerie took place on 3 June 1956. A second stage of construction work was completed on 4 October 1960, an event that coincided with the celebrations for the 400th anniversary of the Staatliche Kunstsammlungen in Dresden. Although the bulk of the holdings survived the war, there were a number of serious losses. In 1963 the Staatliche Kunstsammlungen produced a catalogue documenting the war losses of the Dresden Gemäldegalerie, including all the irretrievably lost paintings by masters old and new, and simultaneously providing the basis for subsequent efforts to search for lost works. The catalogue lists 206 destroyed and 507 missing paintings, of which more than fifty have since been found and returned.[61]

Since the city's destruction, many citizens of Dresden have experienced a kind of double reality comprised of then and now, a life caught between the pictures they knew of the city's lost beauty and the strongly contrasting present. The paintings of Bernardo Bellotto (cats 28–32) provide a record of the city's historic buildings that continues to serve as the yardstick for all innovation. The Gemäldegalerie with its paintings has become the leitmotif for people's hopes and aspirations, and in its representations of destroyed buildings a substitute for all that has been lost.

From the day it reopened, the collection developed a magnetism that brought some 700,000 visitors to the museum each year. But after about thirty years of such visitor numbers the building was in dire need of repair. In February 1988, it was deemed necessary to refurbish the gallery from top to bottom, a project that could be optimised thanks to the new political and economic possibilities opened up by the reunification of Germany. Apart from the refurbishment of the buildings

Fig. 19
The interior of the Gemäldegalerie Alte Meister showing Raphael's *Sistine Madonna* and, in the foreground, Correggio's *Madonna with St George*

and the installation of state-of-the-art technical facilities, a major part of the work focused on restoring the interior decoration scheme of the Semper era in order to preserve an important part of Dresden's heritage. A similarly authentic approach was also borne in mind for the new hang of the paintings, which are now often in two horizontal rows and thus much closer together than in previous years, although by no means as densely packed as during the nineteenth century. Over 2,000 works were on view in the Semperbau when it was opened in 1855; since the reopening on 5 December 1992 some 730 paintings are on display.[62]

More attention has been given to the colours of the walls in order to create a specific character for each room and to distinguish between various sections: Italian paintings hang on a red ground, Dutch and Flemish on green, Spanish and seventeenth-century French on grey. In certain rooms historic colour schemes were reinstated, as in the vestibule and the main staircase, in the Bellotto Corridor and the South Gallery (Room 121), as well as in the German Room (Room 107) in the Zwinger, which also contains the old Netherlandish masters.

The renovation of 1988–92 was largely a response to technical necessity. But there was also a deeper issue involved: in Dresden, whose appalling losses during the war may be the very reason why the feeling for history is so alive in the city, a solution was sought that would continue in the best traditions of museums while at the same time doing justice to the present. Since the reopening, some 400,000 visitors have come to admire this unique collection every year. We are captivated by the paintings of the so-called old masters because the fates and hopes, the experiences and dreams of whole ages live on in them; because, as Louis Aragon remarked in 1956 during his conversations with Jean Cocteau in Paris after the paintings were returned to Dresden, they are 'the mirror of man'.[63] It is these works to which Dresden is indebted for its place among 'Europe's most privileged cities'.

Endnotes

1 Lindau 1885, p. 532.

2 Lindau 1856.

3 Lindau 1883.

4 Cf. Kolb 2002.

5 Cf. Holzhausen 1927; Menzhausen 1985; Vötsch 2002; Watenabe-O'Kelly 2002.

6 Beutel 1671.

7 Cf. Haake 1927; Czok 1989.

8 Cf. Munich 1990.

9 Posse 1937B, p. 11.

10 Cf. Hantzsch 1902.

11 Cf. Heres 1991A.

12 Cf. Oelsner and Prinz 1985.

13 Cited from Heres 1982; Keyssler 1751.

14 Cf. Heres 1983.

15 Cf. Staszewski 1996.

16 Cf. Leiden 2001.

17 Cf. Weber 1994.

18 Purchases made in Paris were by no means simply of French paintings; many Dutch paintings were bought there too. See Dijon 2001.

19 Cf. Heres 1991A, pp. 125, 126.

20 Cf. Winkler 1989.

21 Cf. Dresden 2000C.

22 Cf. Ferrara 2002.

23 Cf. Marx 1999A.

24 Cf. Schramm 1744, p. 244.

25 Heineken 1753–57.

26 Hasche 1781–83, vol. 2, p. 77.

27 Johann Wolfgang von Goethe, Dichtung und Wahrheit, book 8. Goethe visited the gallery while he was a student in Leipzig.

28 Private art collections existed in Dresden during the time of Augustus the Strong. We know that Count Jacob Heinrich von Flemming (1667–1728) and Count Christoph August von Wackerbarth (1662–1634) not only found paintings for the king, but also had their own collections. Flemming's palace, however, was full of paintings belonging to Augustus. Cf. Stübel 1924–25.

29 Cf. Heres 1991B.

30 Cf. Dittrich 1991; Marx 2001.

31 Cf. Stübel 1912, pp. 138ff.

32 Stübel 1912, p. 208. Cf. also Michel 2001.

33 Hagedorn/Baden 1797.

34 Hagedorn/Baden 1797, p. 5.

35 For more details on Hagedorn and the artists Christian Hilfgott Brand (1694–1756), Joseph Orient (1677–1747), Augustus Querfurt (1696–1761) and Ádám Mányocki (1673–1757), cf. Cremer 1989.

36 Hagedorn/Baden 1797, p. 5.

37 Gal. no. 2083.

38 Cf. Bianconi 1781, pp. 16ff.

39 Cf. Marx 2002A.

40 Cf. Schlechte 1992.

41 Schlechte 1992, pp. 44ff.

42 Winckelmann/Rehm 1968, p. 29.

43 Heineken 1753–57; cf. also Marx 1999B.

44 Cited from Winckelmann/Rehm 1968, p. 29.

45 Schäfer 1860, vol. 1, pp. 115ff.

46 Cf. Marx 2000A.

47 Woermann 1887, p. 21. For more on the Lorenzo di Credi, see Weber 1995.

48 For more on Matthäi cf. Dresden 1990, pp. 90, 91.

49 See 'Aus Julius Schnorrs Tagebüchern', Dresdener Geschichtsblätter, 4, 1895, on how the paintings were hung in the Semperbau under the direction of Julius Schnorr von Carolsfeld in 1855.

50 For more on Hübner see Monschau-Schmittmann 1993.

51 Cf. Seydewitz 1957, p. 394.

52 Weinart 1777, p. 308.

53 Cf. Casanova 1984, vol. 3, p. 227. Cf. also Marx 2000B, p. 59.

54 Gessner 1787/88 (1801).

55 Runge 1981, pp. 76, 238.

56 Rethel 1912, p. 66.

57 Cf. Kramer 1916.

58 Cf. Zimmermann 1987.

59 Cf. Seydewitz 1957, pp. 208–15; Petropoulos 1999.

60 Cf. Akinscha and Koslow 1995.

61 Cf. Dresden 1998.

62 Cf. Marx 1993.

63 Aragon and Cocteau 1957, p. 9.

The German School

1

Albrecht Dürer (Nuremberg 1471 – Nuremberg 1528)
Portrait of Bernhard von Reesen, 1521

Inscribed at centre, close
to the upper edge: 1521, with
beneath the artist's
monogram AD; three lines
vertically on the letter:
Dem(...)/ pernh(...)/ zw(...)

Oil on oak panel,
45.5 × 31.5 cm

Probably acquired in 1743 by
Le Leu for Augustus III in
Paris; Dresden inventory
1754, no. 713

Gal. no. 1871

LITERATURE
Woermann 1884/85. Tietze
and Tietze-Conrat 1937/38,
vol. 2, p. 24, no. 810.
Panofsky 1948, pp. 210ff.,
cat. 64. Brand 1970–71,
pp. 59–83. Marx, in
Washington 1978, pp. 219ff.,
no. 537. Anzelewsky 1991,
text vol. p. 265, cat. 163.

Dürer must have painted this vivid portrait of a young man during his travels to the Netherlands, which ended in August 1521, because the panel he used is of oak, a material favoured there but unusual in Nuremberg. The letter the man holds, which is addressed in German, tells us his first name, Bernhard, and allows a reference to be made here to a passage in Dürer's travel diary entered after 16 March 1521 in Antwerp: 'Have likewise portrayed Bernhart von Resten in oils. For this he gave me 8 gulden.' Bernhard von Reesen, a merchant born in 1491 in Danzig who had made his home in Antwerp and was to die shortly after sitting at the end of 1521, was probably the man who sat for this portrait, for which he paid a less than extortionate price.

By choosing the half-length format, in which the sitter's hands appear to rest on the lower part of the frame, Dürer has deliberately followed fifteenth-century Netherlandish tradition. Although this scheme had long since established itself in southern Germany and was well-known to the young Dürer, it seems likely in this case that he returned to it quite consciously, as a kind of enquiry into the customs of his host country. The narrow, almost box-like space on which the shadow of the sitter appears to fall to the right, and the shadow of the frame from above, can also be found in both earlier and contemporary Netherlandish portraiture, in the work of, say, Quinten Massys. The warm reddish-brown of the background is also reminiscent of the Netherlands. It dominates the limited and extremely powerful palette used for the picture, contrasting solely with the twin poles of black and white while seeming to mingle with the latter to produce the flesh tones.

Although the correspondence in Bernhard's hands makes him appear to be a great merchant accustomed to operating over long distances, his distinguished yet not ornate clothing is that of a bourgeois tradesman. His hat is dark, almost black, as are both his gown, trimmed with black fur, and his doublet, which shows his white pleated shirt. The painting gains in both firmness and dynamism from the powerful diagonal that extends from the lower left and up across his shoulder, the shaded line of his cheekbone, and his hat. This large, almost planar-looking garment allows his head to stand out strongly, while also keeping it anchored to the surface. Dürer explores the plasticity of the broad, strong-boned head in a subtle, gentle way that brings out details without losing the overall context. The painter presents his sitter in a narrow, partial view; the absence of the edges of the hat seems to bring him closer to us. But the viewer is unable to establish any contact with the sitter, however tangible his almost front-lit face may seem. Although, with their sharp reflections, the eyes seem alert, the young man's gaze is directed into the middle distance, which gives him a pensive, self-absorbed look. This self-containment lends the picture – despite the marked sensuality of its surface – something of the character of a monument. SK

2

Barthel Beham (?) (Nuremberg 1502 – Italy 1540)

Portrait of a Man with a Black Cap in His Hand, c.1525/30

Oil on lime wood panel,
61.5 × 45.5 cm
(including the 1.3 cm-wide
slat on all sides)

Inv. Dresden 1722–28, A 99;
Riedel and Wenzel 1765,
no. 70

Gal. no. 1905

LITERATURE
Weizsäcker 1900, pp.313ff.,
no. 72. Feuchtmayr 1921.
Feuchtmayr 1928, p.125.
Deusch and Winkler 1935,
p.19, no. 86. Fudickar 1942,
p.43. Osten 1973. Marx, in
Washington 1978, p.219,
no. 536. Marx 1999A, p.274.

NOTES
1 Bätschmann and Griener
1997, pp.134–46.
2 Schmid's opinion,
conveyed in Weizsäcker
1900, p.314; similarly
Feuchtmayr 1921, and
already expressing doubts
Feuchtmayr 1928, p.125.
3 Löcher 1999, pp.75–79,
207, no. 57.

This exceptional portrait depicts a heavily built man, already advanced in years, in front of a pale blue sky with patches of white cloud. Neither his tightly fastened dark olive-green gown with its black fur lining and narrow collar, nor his dark-grey doublet with a glimpse of white-frilled shirt cuffs, nor even his black cap, give any indication of his profession. He might be a cleric, or maybe a scholar, but neither interpretation is conclusive: a simple gown of this kind, like the one in which Luther was portrayed, is also worn by the Catholic former Mayor of Basle, Jakob Meyer zum Hasen, in the *Darmstadt Madonna* by Hans Holbein the Younger.[1] The conjecture that the sitter in the current portrait was a leading figure in spiritual and moral realms has been fed by the work's immediate, petitioning character: the figure towers up before the horizon, which can vaguely be discerned below his shoulder-line, to rise as it were above us. The panel is unable to contain his broad frame at its two sides. The man stands directly before us, front on, his gaze firmly set on the viewer, with none of the relief that might be brought by a slight turn of the head or body. This is all the more compelling because his stern, powerfully sculpted face has immense presence. It seems to extend outwards from the flat background of the painting, and to be almost real in its detailed structure. There can be no doubt that this very rare full-frontal format was not selected here by chance; the direct, presumably moral appeal to the viewer must have been intended. The similarly unusual motif of the cap in hand held in front of the body, hard to interpret but presumably a form of deference, could be viewed in this context as a gesture of humility aimed at intensifying the moral petition.

These qualities once led the picture to be viewed as a portrait of Martin Luther's father, and then in around 1800 as the great reformer himself. The artist was initially identified as Hans Holbein the Younger, but by 1817 the catalogue gave the artist as an anonymous early German painter. This description has prevailed to the present day; Gert von der Osten's attempt to credit it to Wolf Huber has been dismissed. On the other hand, around 1900 Heinrich Alfred Schmid and Heinrich Weizsäcker discerned the same hand in this painting as in the portrait of the Bavarian chamberlain Hans Urmiller in the Städelsche Kunstinstitut in Frankfurt.[2] Their suggestion has for a long time been largely overlooked, but it seems correct: there is the greatest possible kinship between the moulding of the face and hands in the two paintings, as well as in the actual manner of painting. Assuming that Kurt Löcher is correct in attributing the Urmiller portrait to the Nuremberg-born Munich painter Barthel Beham,[3] as is now generally accepted, the Dresden work must also be from his brush. In that case this enthralling portrait would, like the Urmiller portrait, be one of the outstanding works of Beham's incomparable *oeuvre*. SK

3

Lucas Cranach the Elder (Kronach 1472 – Weimar 1553)

Elector John the Constant of Saxony, 1526

Inscribed on the right above the shoulder with the winged serpent and dated 1526

Oil on lime wood panel, 57 × 37 cm

1931 from the House of Wettin, collection Prince George of Saxony; in the night of 27/28 April 1945 from the Albrechtsburg Meissen to a place of concealment, Pockau-Lengefeld; according to the report of restorer Unger still in Pockau-Lengefeld on 5 May 1945, then disappeared; returned to the Gemäldegalerie on 6 December 1967 by the USSR Ministry of Culture

Gal. no. 1908 B

LITERATURE
Schuchardt 1851, vol. 2, p.54, no. 288. Dresden 1899, pp.34ff., no. 26. Posse 1932, pp.73ff. Posse 1942, pp.63ff., no.102. Ebert 1963, p.86, no.1908 B. Dresden 1971, p.107, no. 113. Friedländer and Rosenberg 1989, pp. 130ff., no.311. Hoffmann 1992, p.40. Dresden 1998, p. 145, no.8.

NOTES
1 Hoffmann 1992, p.40.
2 Posse 1932, pp.73–74.

John the Constant (1468–1532) was a member of the Ernestine line of the House of Wettin. During the lifetime of his brother, Elector Frederick the Wise, he became involved in the business of government. After his brother's death in 1525, John the Constant inherited the position of Elector and became Cranach's new master, in which role he proved no less benevolent than Frederick the Wise.

One of Cranach's main duties as court painter consisted in portraying the Saxon princes as well as their families and allies. The portraits were not only intended as documentation of the line of descent for royal ancestral galleries, but also as gifts. The mutual exchange of portraits was a court custom, with the result that we know what John the Constant looked like from a number of paintings by Cranach. Two further portraits of the Elector of a comparable size to the Dresden painting and based on the same design are known: one, also inscribed with the date 1526, is now in the keeping of the Kröller-Müller Collection in Otterlo, while another in the Schlossmuseum in Weimar can be dated in all certainty to *c.* 1526.[1]

The present half-length portrait shows John the Constant in semi-profile at the age of 58. His arms are elided on the left and right edges of the painting, but the work's narrow format lends the portrait an expression of monumental immediacy. Moreover, the sitter stands out by virtue of the signet ring on his left hand, the chain around his neck bearing several rings and a small cross, and above all the rich embroidery on his shirt collar and the precious fur trim on his gown. The garland of carnations in his hair, traditionally worn at weddings, prompted Hans Posse to conjecture in 1932 that the portrait might have been painted on the occasion of the betrothal of the sitter's son, John Frederick the Generous, to Sibylle of Cleves in 1526, and that the Elector is depicted here as the father of the groom.[2] This thesis is supported by two portraits in the Schlossmuseum in Weimar that Cranach also painted in 1526, showing John Frederick and the princess as a bridal couple; these are in the same format as the current depiction of John the Constant. KK

Monogrammist AB

Scenes from the Childhood of Jesus, *c.* 1530

The Annunciation
Oil on lime wood panel,
42 × 39.1 cm

The Visitation
Monogram on the cornice
above Mary to the right
Oil on lime wood panel,
41.5 × 38.6 cm (slightly
cropped at the upper
and right-hand edges)

The Birth of Jesus
Monogram in the keystone
of the arch
Oil on lime wood panel,
41.5 × 39.5 cm

The Adoration of the Magi
Monogram on the golden
casket being presented
by the kneeling king
Oil on lime wood panel,
42 × 39 cm

Mentioned in a supplement
to the inventory of the
Kunstkammer from 1595
(f. 361b); 1832 to the
Gemäldegalerie

Not restored during the last
fifty years; labels attached
to the reverse of the panels
document the cleaning of
the paintings and the filling
of wormholes by Gallery
Inspector Renner in 1840

Gal. nos 1896–1898, 1900

LITERATURE
Matthäi 1835, p.21, nos
89–93. Dresden 1846, p.57,
nos 472–76. Woermann 1887,
Gal. nos 1896–1900. Posse
1930, p.137, nos 1896–1900.
Thieme/Becker 1907–50,
vol. 37, p.372. Dresden
2000C, pp.68ff., cat. 9.

NOTES
1 Dresden 2000C, p.68.
2 Winkler 1964, pp.141ff.

Three of the five Dresden *Scenes from the Childhood of Jesus* are signed with the monogram AB, similar to Dürer's famous monogram. The device is also to be found on a sixth panel which was recognised in 1929 as belonging to the series, a *Flight into Egypt*, which found its way in *1922/24* from the Brocard Collection to the Pushkin Museum in Moscow. The sequence is regarded as a *Life of the Virgin*, although only the story of Jesus's childhood is told, while specific events in the life of Mary, such as the birth of the Mother of God, her death, ascension and coronation, are missing.

Apart from an *Adoration of the Magi* credited to AB that was part of the Hohenzollern Collection in Sigmaringen until 1894 whose present whereabouts are unknown, no further works by this artist are known. Although the sequence went under the name 'unknown' in 1835, 1837 and 1838 and subsequently – due to the monogram – was erroneously attributed to Augustin Braun, a contemporary of Rubens in Cologne, since 1887 the painter has been given in the Dresden catalogues as a Swabian. Yet the broadness of Mary's face and her narrow eyes and full cheeks indicate that the artist trained under Lucas Cranach the Elder. A more concrete indication of this surmise is to be found in Cranach the Elder's work from around 1525. Like the Monogrammist, the Cranach workshop had repeatedly adopted the less usual night scene for the Nativity, as can be seen in the painting in the Dresden Gemäldegalerie (Gal. no. 1907 A). Likewise indicative of Cranach is the representation of the angels as naked winged putti: this motif is used in isolated cases by other artists, but Cranach employed it for a large variety of subjects, including a depiction of the Man of Sorrows in Dresden (Gal. no. 1914). A love of atmospheric effects – the *Adoration of the Magi* and the *Flight into Egypt* both have impressive winter backdrops – the extreme use of perspective in the *Birth of Jesus* and the *Circumcision* and various isolated adaptations from the style of the Danube School were in all probability mediated by Cranach, one of the school's leading representatives. A particularly impressive example of such perspectival depth can be seen in the *Birth of the Virgin* in the St Anne altar in Feldkirch painted in 1521 by Wolf Huber, another specialist in early snowscapes. The use of lime wood for the panel was also common in the Cranach workshop, so nothing more need stand in the way of attributing these paintings to the same or a neighbouring circle of artists. The model used for Mary in the *Annunciation* has also been detected in the region, albeit in a much cruder form, in the central panels of the St Mary altar in Winteritz. Moreover, Birgit Kloppenburg has noted that the early mention of the panels in the Kunstkammer also speaks in favour of their coming from Saxony. In addition, the style of both Mary's dress and her hair in the *Birth of Jesus* recalls Cranach.[1]

The fact that the artist was open to other sources of inspiration is underlined by the figure of Elizabeth in the *Visitation*. Her severe profile is almost reminiscent of the Florentine Renaissance, although it would appear in this case to have come from the Upper Rhine, or indeed from Swabia, the region formerly thought to be the origin of the artist. The outline and cut of Elizabeth's garments – to just below the waist – are almost completely identical to those of the daughter in Holbein the Younger's *Meyer Madonna*, of which the Dresden Gemäldegalerie has a famous copy (Gal. no. 1892). The profile of the angel of the *Annunciation* has similar echoes,

although in this case of much earlier works from the Holbein family – namely those of Hans Holbein the Elder. Resemblances in the firmness and volume of the bodies to the later Hans Suess of Kulmbach, the later Barthel Beham, or to Georg Pencz seem, on the other hand, more the result of a general *Zeitgeist* than of concrete personal or geographical links. As with these Nuremberg painters, the figures have abandoned all the delicacy and exaggerated feeling of movement of Gothicism, a step that the Monogrammist has taken to the extreme with his broad, bell-like silhouettes.

A mutual stimulus for these formal tendencies is no doubt to be found in Italy. The gentle transitions between forms, the pensive expression on many of the faces, the motifs such as the transparent scarf on the head of Mary in the *Visitation* – here shown as a buxom matron – point to the influence of Leonardo da Vinci throughout European painting at that time. Extending from Joos van Cleve in the Netherlands to Vicente Macip in Spanish Valencia, this widespread phenomenon cannot be viewed as a specific debt here. It is sufficient to compare the profile of the woman on the far left of the *Circumcision* and the cut of the scarf over her head with the holy women in the *Birth of the Virgin* or the *Crucifixion* by Macip on the high altar of the cathedral at Segorbe to illustrate the range of Leonardo's influence. Although the compositional idea of placing a figure in profile at the edge of the scene, and then combining it with a second, auxiliary figure turned towards the first and thus away from central events, is also found in its inception in Schongauer or Dürer, it is basically an artistic device that was widely used in Italy, from Lippi to Raphael and Leonardo. Additionally, the fondness for figures in profile points generally to the stimulation that came from beyond the Alps, as does the restraint shown in the gestures: both the Angel of the Annunciation as well as the celebrant in the *Circumcision*, who is based on the same fundamental pattern, genuflect with both knees on the ground, and the banderole with its two gently curling ends slips evenly from the hands of the angel. Similarly, the pale coloration, which was to become even more evident after the removal of the yellowed varnish, fits this scenario.

The possibility that these ideas and associations give for dating the series to the years around 1530 – and not later, to the second third or even the second half of the sixteenth century, as the old Dresden catalogues (1887 or 1905, and 1920 or 1930)

The Circumcision, *c.* 1530.
Oil on lime wood panel,
41.9 x 39 cm. Gal. no. 1899

41

had it – receives more concrete corroboration in the form of Joseph's beard, for instance, which is broad and trimmed straight at the bottom, or from the costume worn by Elizabeth in the *Visitation*. Some forms, above all the throne in the circumcision scene and the fluting in the frieze on the wall of the visitation scene, already display the effects of the Renaissance, which arrived early in Saxony. But even as an echo of the Renaissance, the choice of German for the text on the angel's banderole is unusual; the hint of dialect in the words '[G]EGRVSET SEISTU HOLDSE…R' (Hail to thee sweet…R) must be borne in mind when fixing the sequence to a region.

In the visitation scene, Elizabeth is placed beside Mary like a piece of theatre scenery, an impression that is almost strengthened by the gesture she makes to the child in Mary's body. Likewise, some of the other compositions give the impression that the artist took outside models for his inspiration, in most cases from prints. Against this, the preliminary outlines, which show through in numerous places and differ from the finished work, demonstrate that he did not adhere to his models in a pedantic way. Moreover, apart from the occasional detail, the only case in which an already existent visual idea has been adopted is the *Birth of Jesus*. As already mentioned, this painting picks up on the popular sixteenth-century idea of setting the scene at night and letting the crib be illuminated by the child himself, thus underlining his divine nature all the more forcefully, especially when contrasted with the weaker, more mundane light of Joseph's candle. The idea for the picture seems to come from the Netherlands, although scarcely from Hugo van der Goes, as Friedrich Winkler again maintained in 1964.[2] Indeed, other than is suggested when the idea is falsely accredited to Michel Sittow, for instance, this winsome, almost sentimental image tends to have been adopted in the Netherlands by second- or third-rate artists; in Germany, by contrast, it was employed by leading lights such as Baldung, Barthel Bruyn, Holbein the Younger, Altdorfer or indeed Lucas Cranach the Elder. Thus the nocturnal *Birth of Jesus* in the Dresden cycle cannot be taken to indicate that the artist was strongly influenced by the Netherlands, as has constantly but erroneously been claimed for the Monogrammist ever since Friedrich Matthäi's Dresden catalogue of 1835.

In the same way that German painters generally introduced more formal variation to their subjects than their Netherlandish colleagues, the Monogrammist avoids any slavish adherence to the prevailing models. Although he is by no means totally consistent in his methods, he even manages to derive a special charm from the light effects, as in the shadow cast by the manger on the wall. Highly curious, however, is the idea of bedding the baby Jesus down in what resembles the side of a barrel, so that his divine effulgence may radiate all the more freely. It is no coincidence that the somewhat maudlin nineteenth century saw the panels being taken out of storage and placed before the general public; in his first mention of the works in 1835 Friedrich Matthäi explicitly states, 'curiously enough the light in this picture [radiates] from the child far more ingeniously and naturally than in the *Holy Night* by Correggio'.

Indeed, it is precisely in the secondary details that the Monogrammist is so refreshingly independent and inventive. The *Visitation* was regularly depicted before a magnificent estate with moats and bridges, but rarely were Mary and Elizabeth to be seen on a wooden slat bridge with a handrail spanning a stream; a second bridge has later to be crossed in the Moscow *Flight into Egypt*. The artist was keen on the correctness of the details in the materials: he shows the individual planks that make up the rear of the throne in the *Circumcision*, leaves the masonry in the heavy stone pillars of the church interior exposed, and has braces to attach the lead beading to the wooden mullion and transom in the rose window at the back. In the *Adoration of the Magi*, the icicles have been located at the joints between the individual roof tiles, and the overall formation playfully echoes the pleats in the gown of the youngest king and the rippling row of pelts in the collar of the oldest. For the

Flight into Egypt, Joseph carries a cradle on his back fitted with runners and handles on its sides. As in the *Circumcision*, he holds a stripping iron in place of a staff, identifying himself as a carpenter. Finally, in the *Annunciation* the Monogrammist emphasises the locked wooden door with its cased lock which has failed to prevent the supernatural visitor from entering. The heavy curtain that covers the open balustrade behind Mary has been raised and draped over a cloak-hook to provide space for Mary and the descending baby Jesus.

It has yet to be clarified how and where the panels were to be mounted, but the material they are made of allows certain conclusions to be drawn. Unusual here is the incoming light from the right, which may have been chosen to lend extra emphasis to the supernatural light effects in the *Birth of Jesus*. It follows that the panels were never painted on both sides, and thus could not have been part of a winged altar that could be opened and closed. The reverses have simply been given a quick smooth-down and a coat of lead white. A groove runs around the rear edge of each panel, so the possibility can be excluded that the works – which mostly consist of a single board – were sawn apart at some later date. In keeping with this, a strip of grounded but unpainted wood has been left exposed on the lower edge of the *Adoration*.

Following the narrative and form of the panels, the pictures can be grouped as pairs. The *Annunciation* and the *Visitation* can be placed together solely on the strength of their depictions of the sky; the *Birth of Jesus* and the *Circumcision* are linked by their dim light and their use of strongly receding perspective; and the *Adoration* and the *Flight* are united by their winter scenery. Doors, walls or furniture round off the pictures on their outer edges. Although we should not expect the painter to be absolutely consistent in such matters, he has shifted the vanishing point of all six works away from the central axis towards its partner panel. Whether the three pairs of pictures were meant to be arranged as a single whole, or to be supplemented by other panels, and whether they were to be arranged in several vertical rows, or were intended for a non-movable retable or for wall niches, will remain far more difficult to answer. It is worth remembering, however, that scarcely sixty years after they were painted the panels were already part of a royal art cabinet. It can furthermore be established that they were already mounted in individual black frames, and that by then the *Flight*, now in Moscow, had already been separated from the sequence.
MW

The Flight into Egypt.
c. 1530. Oil on lime wood panel, 43.5 x 39 cm. Pushkin Museum, Moscow

Lucas Cranach the Younger (Wittenberg 1515 – Wittenberg 1586)

Adam and Eve, after 1537

Eve inscribed lower right
with the symbol of the
winged serpent

Oil on lime wood panel,
each 171 × 63 cm

Probably came via Elector
Johann Georg II to the
Kunstkammer in 1657; from
there to the Gemäldegalerie;
first found in the inventory
of 1722–28: B 250 (Eve),
B 253 (Adam)

Gal. no. 1916 A
Gal. no. 1916 A A

LITERATURE
Schuchardt 1851, vol. 2,
p. 42, nos 228, 229. Lindau
1883, pp. 223ff. Friedländer
and Rosenberg 1932,
p. 82, no. 288. Zurich 1971,
p. 47. Berlin 1983, p. 301.
Friedländer and Rosenberg
1989, p. 141, no. 357. Schoen
2001, p. 204.

NOTES
1 On the relationship
  between Cranach and
  Dürer see most recently
  Schoen 2001, pp. 195–212.
2 Inv. Dresden 1754, Riedel
  and Wenzel 1765 and
  Riedel 1801.
3 'Lucas Cranach le
  vieux…a laissé plusieurs
  ouvrages d'un grand fini,
  quoique fort peu correct
  dans le dessein & d'un
  goût gothique', Lehninger
  1782, pp. 245–46.

This depiction by Lucas Cranach the Younger of the founders of the human race was part of a tradition in the Cranach workshop that spanned many decades. Lucas Cranach the Elder had produced a number of variants from 1509 onwards. Apart from small-sized versions on panel, we know of life-size pairs of paintings, of which the Gemäldegalerie Alte Meister in Dresden possesses not only those presented here, but also a pair by Lucas Cranach the Elder from 1531 (Gal. nos 1911, 1912). Albrecht Dürer's first independent formulations of this theme in 1504 and 1507 were certainly the inspiration for Cranach's work on the subject. But unlike Dürer, Cranach was less interested in Antiquity and classical proportions, and operated rather within north Alpine traditions that were strongly influenced by Burgundian-Dutch forms.[1]

Cranach's fundamental principle of varying individual motifs is illustrated in his depictions of Adam and Eve. Not only the posture and the vocabulary of gestures, but also the positioning of the fig-leaves, the background design and the representations of the animals can be found in either similar or identical form in the various versions that came from the Cranach workshop. Thus the way Adam touches his head with his left hand can already be found in Cranach the Elder's *Adam and Eve* of 1526 (Courtauld Institute of Art, London). The method of combining individual components to produce a striking overall impression gives a special quality to the Cranachs' works, which are never mere copies of previous designs.

General interest in the nude made the subject of Adam and Eve popular during the sixteenth century; in subsequent years it had an effect on the choice of the Dresden Gemäldegalerie's acquisitions and exhibitions. In the Gemäldegalerie on Jüdenhof, which became the permanent home of the royal collection for over a century until its move in 1855 to the newly built Sempergalerie, only six paintings from the Cranach workshop were on view between 1754 and 1805.[2] But in every case they consisted of life-size pairs of paintings depicting nudes: *Adam and Eve* by Lucas Cranach the Elder (Gal. nos 1911, 1912), the *Adam and Eve* shown here by Lucas Cranach the Younger, and *Judith and Lucretia* (Gal. no. 1916, war loss), which is also given to Cranach the Elder. So for over fifty years only these three pairs of pictures were deemed worthy of public view, while other works by the Cranachs were felt to be 'not very correctly drawn and of a Gothic flavour'.[3] From 1806 onwards, other Cranach paintings were gradually integrated into the works on display, but a genuine re-evaluation of early German painting as a whole was only to begin with the Romantics. KK

10

Adam Elsheimer (Frankfurt am Main 1578 – Rome 1610)

Jupiter and Mercury at the House of Philemon and Baucis, *c.1608/09*

Oil on copper,
16.5 × 22.5 cm

First mentioned in the 1754
inventory, II, 679

Gal. no. 1977

LITERATURE
Frankfurt 1966, no. 38.
Andrews 1985, pp. 35, 189,
no. 24. Dresden 1992, p. 191.
Munich 1998, p. 465. Warnke
1999, pp. 392–97.

NOTES
1 Warnke sees rather the
  union of two stylistic
  modes in this picture;
  Warnke 1999, pp. 396ff.
2 Cited in Andrews 1985,
  p. 54.

Adam Elsheimer's early works were still clearly in the tradition of sixteenth-century painting and printmaking; yet at the same time the Flemish landscape painters working in Frankenthal were also an important influence on him. In 1598 he travelled to Venice; from around 1600 he is known to have been in Rome; and in 1606 he was admitted to the Accademia di San Luca in that city, where he was able to explore the works of contemporary artists such as Caravaggio or Paul Bril.

From 1606/07 he produced a number of paintings based on episodes from the *Metamorphoses* by the Roman author Ovid, including the story of *Jupiter and Mercury at the House of Philemon and Baucis*. The two gods wandered the face of the earth in human guise; finally, after being constantly turned away from more affluent households, they were taken in by the old, happily married couple Philemon and Baucis. The couple spared no effort to make their guests feel at home, initially failing to recognise them as gods. In their gratitude, Jupiter and Mercury saved them from the floods and general destruction that befell the world about them. Their hut was transformed into a temple, and the married couple chose to serve in it as priests. And instead of either of them having to grieve at the death of the other, the two were simultaneously transformed into trees at the end of their joint life.

In Elsheimer's day, the story would have been read as a parable of divine revelation to humanity, most especially to the poor, and as having strong analogies with Biblical tales. The painter does not show the transformation, but rather concentrates on the hospitality extended to the gods by the married couple, as is described at length in Ovid, and more specifically on the events before the meal. The low door and the cramped space inside the hut, the bed covered with its simple covers, the care and attention showered on the guests – Elsheimer takes all this from Ovid and presents it, enriched by a couple of motifs of his own, to the viewer. Even the goose, which the aged couple intended to slaughter for the wanderers and that was spared at the gods' behest, can be seen in the foreground. Elsheimer's estate contained a copy of the *Metamorphoses*, and it is clear that he read it carefully. Among the inventions not from Ovid but unique to the painting is a picture on the wall, probably a coloured print. On examining an engraving taken from the painting, Goethe considered that the print showed one of Jupiter's 'amorous pranks performed with Mercury's aid'. There may well be a streak of humour in the way that Jupiter's gaze glides over the picture. At the same time, this picture within a picture reflects the very function of the cabinet picture we are looking at. Its iconography, however, is more indebted to the ordinary standards of mythological representation at that time, and thus emphasises the unique quality of Elsheimer's interior.[1]

By situating the scene indoors, Elsheimer's depiction differs strongly from the admittedly rare earlier examples of this subject. The artificial light sources are given special significance: to the left, an oil lamp brightens the faces of the gods and lends them additional force; to the right, a somewhat weaker light illuminates in particular the still-life in the foreground. In this the picture matches a series of nocturnes that Elsheimer painted during the same period in Rome with the aim of mastering the techniques of Caravaggio. The German painter and art theorist Joachim von Sandrart considered this work's use of chiaroscuro to be quite exemplary; as we read in his *Academie* of 1675, Elsheimer painted the present work after finishing another, successful nocturne, and shows in it how, 'fatigued by their travels, Jupiter and Mercurius entered the lowly farmhouse of Pausae and Philemonis and sat by the lamplight, which provided sufficient illumination for them and these poor people and their chattels, so that this and the following work is a meet lesson and education from which one may learn and be inspired to do justice to night scenes, and I confess that in my youth, when I began to paint, I too took this as an ideal, guideline and formula'.[2]

This small cabinet painting, on copper like many of Elsheimer's works, was disseminated in engravings and copies, and even Rembrandt was to draw inspiration from it. EH

11

Abraham Mignon (Frankfurt am Main 1640 – Utrecht 1679)
A Glass with Flowers and an Orange Twig, 1660s

Signed lower left:
A. Mignon. fe.

Oil on canvas,
88 × 67 cm

First in Dresden
inv. 1722–28, A 196

Gal. no. 2017

LITERATURE
Noble 1972, pp. 11ff., 25ff.,
39ff. Dresden 1983, pp. 138ff.
Gemar-Koeltzsch 1995,
vol. 3, pp. 668.

Abraham Mignon was born in 1640, the son of French-Reformed emigrants living in Frankfurt am Main. There he became the pupil of Jacob Marrel, who had himself studied under Georg Flegel and Jan Davidsz de Heem. Mignon accompanied his teacher on a number of journeys to Holland, finally moving in 1667 to Utrecht, where he joined de Heem's studio and in 1669 became a member of the St Lukas Guild. Mignon, whose work consists primarily of flower and fruit pieces, is classified on the strength of his birth and training in Frankfurt am Main as a representative of German painting, but he can also be viewed as a member of the Dutch School if the character of his work and the city in which he pursued his later career are considered.

This still-life, which was painted in the 1660s, shows a bulbous vase resting on a stone ledge. The arrangement in the vase contains a variety of flowers, including roses, carnations, irises, Chinese lanterns and poppies, interspersed with ears of corn, a stalk of blackberries and an orange twig. To the right is a wilting tulip, below which we see gooseberries and a thistle entwined by bindweed. A number of snails and insects, including butterflies and dragonflies, spiders, beetles, ants, bees and caterpillars, inhabit the picture. The thorny stems, magnified by the glass bowl as if by a reading glass, form a strong contrast to the rounded forms of the flowers with their soft, velvety petals.

Mignon's earlier vase paintings allow direct reference to de Heem's flower pieces, both in their arrangements as well as in the distribution of light and colour. In keeping with this, Mignon has arranged the flowers asymmetrically; the three prominent striped tulips create strong accents in the picture's upper half that are offset by the compact motif of the three roses at the left. The blades of grass, ears of corn and blackberry stalks contrast with the full, heavy blooms. Illumination comes from an outside source on the left that lights the canvas almost front on. Most strongly illuminated are the triple-rose motif and the carnation that hangs below the ledge. The monochrome background, which produces scarcely any depth, and the lack of a middleground heighten the plasticity of the flower arrangement in the foreground. A sense of space is further created by the ledge and the reflection of the studio window in the vase.

Seventeenth-century fruit and flower pieces are often interpreted as Vanitas still-lifes, in which the transience of all life is placed before the viewer. In the present example, the wilting flowers and the insects which devour and blight the flowers and fruit should be understood as Vanitas symbols. As so often, these references to transience can only be seen after a closer look at the work.

Mignon's perfect imitation of nature reflects the age of the natural sciences, and specifically the ambition of reproducing visible reality as precisely as possible with brush and paint. His works present excerpts from the world of nature with great scientific precision. The fact that Mignon, an active Calvinist, integrated symbolic elements into his work, as was certainly typical of Dutch flower pieces, can be taken for granted. MS

12

Paul Heermann (Weigmannsdorf, near Freiberg 1673 – Dresden 1732)

King Augustus II of Poland, 1718 or earlier

White marble; pedestal
of grey marble with red
inclusions, renewed c. 1900

Without pedestal 74 cm
(with pedestal 92 cm)
x 66.5 × 27 cm

Signed under the right arm:
PHeermann. Sc.

Purchased 1763 from the
estate of Count Brühl

Skulpturensammlung,
Dresden, Inv. H4 2/6

LITERATURE
Sponsel 1906, p.61, no.132.
Asche 1961, pp.135ff., 172ff.
Seelig 1977, pp.67ff.
Raumschüssel 1987, p.32,
no. 52. Marx, in Columbus
1999, pp.149ff. Stephan 2001,
p.78, no.12.

This magnificent bust depicts King Augustus II of Poland (1670–1733), known as Augustus the Strong, as an energetic and sensuous ruler. The sculptural qualities of his facial structure have been emphasised in a striking manner. The rippling locks of the wig have not been given the compact fullness typical of many rulers' busts from around 1700, but instead have a linear delicacy. Likewise, the drapes of his cloak have been kept relatively flat, so as to emphasise the volumes of the head and focus attention on the face of the king with his lively gaze. Hanging across his cuirass is the sash of the Catholic Polish Order of the White Eagle, which Augustus reintroduced in 1705 as the Order of the House of Wettin, and visible on his cloak above is the order's star. The cross on the latter bears the order's motto: 'PRO FIDE REGE ET LEGE' (For the faith, the king and the law). The cloak has been draped in such a way as to conceal the king's left shoulder; its folds echo the shield-like contour of the bust and allow part of the armour and the beginnings of an arm to show. Together with the powerful turn of the head, this underlines the monarch's enterprising spirit.

Attempts to date the bust have varied from 1713–16 (Sponsel 1906) to 'after 1728' (Raumschüssel 1987), although for a time 'around 1725' seemed to be largely accepted (Seelig 1977). Stephan 2001 rightly notes a temporal proximity to Louis de Silvestre's *portrait d'apparat* of the king showing the insignia of his coronation, which definitely dates from 1718 (Gal. no. 3943). Harald Marx is to be thanked here for an oral communication in which he lent greater precision to the date: such extensive agreement exists between the painting and the bust – in the shape of the armour, the details of the wig, the angle of the head and the approach to the king's physiognomy – that Silvestre must have taken the bust as his model, which would mean that it must have been made in 1718 or slightly earlier. The other possibility, that Heermann modelled his bust after the portrait, is very unlikely, for in none of his other portraits has Silvestre achieved the same immediacy and plasticity. Silvestre returned to the bust a second time for the equestrian portrait of Augustus (Gal. no. 768) painted at around the same time as the 1718 *portrait d'apparat*.

Paul Heermann worked with his uncle George Heermann on the allegorical sculptures for Troja Castle in Prague, a period of work that was interrupted by a stay in Rome around 1700. Heermann is known to have been in Dresden after the completion of these sculptures in 1705; while there he would have seen works by Guillaume Coustou the Elder and François Coudray. As a co-worker in Dresden with Balthasar Permoser he was involved in making the sculptures for the Zwinger, and created a number of other high-quality pieces in the city, not least for the Großer Garten. Of particular interest in connection with this bust is a bronzed plaster model Heermann made for an equestrian statue of Augustus the Strong, showing him mounted on a rearing horse (Skulpturensammlung, Dresden, Inv. Abgüsse ZV 2130). MWo

13
Johann Alexander Thiele (Erfurt 1685 – Dresden 1752)
View of Dresden from the Loessnitz Heights, 1751

Inscribed lower left: Ein extra schöner Prospect, aufgenommen von der Höhe eines Weinbergs, ohnweit Wackerbarths Ruhe, das Gesicht gegen Dresden und Königstein, gemahlt von Alex. Thielen. 1751 [A particularly beautiful prospect, taken from a vineyard not far from Wackerbarths Ruhe, facing Dresden and Königstein, painted by Alex. Thiele. 1751]

Oil on canvas,
103 × 156 cm

Since 1833 in the 'Sammlung vaterländischer Prospecte'; first in the 1862 catalogue of the Gemäldegalerie, no. 1985; 1914 in Schloss Pillnitz; returned after 1945 to the Gemäldegalerie; c. 1999 given back to the former royal family (the Albertine line of the house of Wettin) and purchased the same year for the gallery

Gal. no. 3181

LITERATURE
Matthäi 1834, pp. 39ff., no. 18. Stübel 1914, p. 55, no. 37. Prause 1954, no. 385. Reyher 1961, no. 81. Göpfert 1972, no. 64. Columbus 1999, no. 52. Dresden 2000B, pp. 32, 33. Dijon 2001, no. 5. Hamburg 2002, no. 7. Marx 2002A, no. 36.

NOTE
1 Hagedorn 1762, p. 385.

'Thiele often shows us the no-less beautiful River Elbe, with large tracts of land extending as far as the sharpest eye can see. Nature has elected him as one of her landscapists.'[1] This was how Christian Ludwig von Hagedorn characterised and lauded the painter at the end of a review of depictions of the Rhine, as we know from Herman Saftleven and Jan Griffier.

Our gaze roams from the vineyards on the slopes of Loessnitz into the far distance, where the city of Dresden appears as a silhouette, the tower of the Hofkirche still incomplete. The striking outlines of Alpsandsteingebirge can be seen on the horizon, with the fortress of Königstein standing out most noticeably. Thiele is at the peak of his abilities in this painting: the landscape swings rhythmically with the river and the chains of hills, until the contours all dissolve in the background. A feeling of distance is produced by the dark brown passages at the front. Late seventeenth-century landscapes, such as those of Pieter Gysels, perhaps, may have stimulated this view.

In 1834 Friedrich Matthäi remarked on this painting that 'the interesting things that are revealed to us as we gaze from the lovely Elbe valley to the Bohemian border in the distance are somewhat heightened in size, which should not be criticised here. Harder to excuse is the wallpapery look of the foreground…but one should not be accused of being partisan when one asserts that it stands on a par with the paintings of a Claude Lorrain in its tone and clarity.' Indeed, Thiele's view seems so directly influenced by Claude's *Landscape with the Flight into Egypt* (cat. 37) that we can surmise that the French painting must have arrived in Dresden in precisely the year that Thiele painted his landscape. HM

14

Anton Raphael Mengs (Aussig 1728 – Rome 1779)
The Penitent Magdalene, 1752

Oil on canvas,
47.5 × 63.5 cm

First mentioned as in
Dresden 1756; Riedel
and Wenzel 1765, p.242

Gal. no. 2162

LITERATURE
Schilling 1843–44, vol. 1,
p. 26. Woermann 1894.
Honisch 1960, p.26. Dresden
1976, p.33. Marx, in Florence
1982, p.86, no. II.2. Vienna
1988, no. 25. Marx, in
Munich 1990, no. 29.
Schlechte 1992, p.190. Marx,
in Madrid 1998, no. 26. Marx,
in Columbus 1999, no. 26.
Roettgen 1999, p. 137, no. 90.
Dresden 2001A, no. 39.

NOTES
1 Schlechte 1992, p.190:
  'Mengs le père vint le 29
  août prendre congé de
  moi et me dit que son fils
  venait de produire à
  l'Académie des peintres
  de Rome le Compagnon
  de la Madeleine du
  Corrège, qu'il vient
  d'achever pour le roi, et
  que sur l'applaudisse-
  ment que ce tableau avait
  eu généralement son fils
  avait été élu membre de
  l'Académie.'
2 Dresden, Sächsisches
  Hauptstaatsarchiv, loc.
  676, f. 25. See Roettgen
  2001, no. 39.
3 Roettgen 1993, nos 28, 29.

The depiction of Mary Magdalene as a penitent does not appear in the Bible. It was not until the twelfth century that the legend arose of how she withdrew to a cave in Sainte-Baume in Provence in order to do penance after a life of sin.

Anton Raphael Mengs painted the picture in 1752 in Rome, and it led to his admittance to the Accademia di San Luca. It deliberately contrasts with Correggio's then-famous version of the subject (old copy formerly in Dresden, Gal. no. 154; war loss), and might even draw on another *Penitent Magdalene* once in Dresden by Pompeo Batoni (formerly Dresden, Gal. no. 454; war loss).

The painting is mentioned in the diary of Friedrich Christian, at that time heir to the Elector, on 29 August 1752: 'Father Mengs came on 29 August to take his leave and said that his son had just completed his counterpart to Correggio's Magdalene for the King [Augustus III] and exhibited it at the Academy in Rome; the painting had met with general acclaim and led to his son being elected to the Academy.'[1] In a letter dated 26 July 1756, Count Brühl mentioned the painting and said that it was the only one Mengs had sent to Dresden since his departure for Rome.[2]

Mengs tackled the subject on numerous occasions, and in very different ways. Like Batoni, he painted a John the Baptist as an accompaniment to another portrayal of Mary Magdalene.[3] No such pendant is known for the painting in Dresden.

Elegance and an expression of great sensitivity are combined with reminiscences of sixteenth- and seventeenth-century painting, along with echoes of Classicism in the drapery and the landscape. Particular mention has been made of Titian, not only in reference to the landscape to the right, but also to the figure: 'Titian's portraits of Venus must have served model for this large, almost immobile nude,' remarked Dieter Honisch, before pointing to the influence of Correggio and continuing: 'The fact that Mengs prefers the precious, sentimental expression of Correggio's figures to the coarser pathos of the Baroque makes it evident just how indebted he was to the stylised, courtly sensitivity of the Rococo.' As such, this small work clearly reveals to us the personal style of its author, who was brought up by his father Ismael Mengs to become a painter and urged to copy and 'improve on' the great masters. His very name reveals these wishes: Anton, from Antonio Allegris, called Correggio, stands for a soft blending of colours, while Raphael stands for classically correct draughtsmanship.

Apart from the possible models of Batoni and Correggio, attention should also be drawn to Luca Giordano's *Penitent Magdalene* in the Dresden Gemäldegalerie (Gal. no. 478). For all the differences between the Giordano and the Mengs, there are far clearer parallels between them than with the two paintings that have always been compared to the Mengs until now: the diagonal alignment of the figure, for instance, or the head propped on one hand, the drape consisting solely of a length of cloth, the right leg, or even the landscape. One noticeable difference is, however, that Mengs's Magdalene is reading a scroll, while in Giordano's painting she leans one arm on a skull that rests on a book. The origin of the Giordano is still unclear; its presence in Dresden was only documented much later. The 1835 catalogue mentions it without any acquisition details. Its attribution at that time to Francesco Solimena was amended in 1843 in the light of the hitherto unnoticed signature. HM

15

Caspar David Friedrich (Greifswald 1774 – Dresden 1840)

Bohemian Landscape with Mount Milleschauer, 1808

Oil on canvas,
70 × 104 cm

1921 from Count Franz von
Thun-Hohenstein, Tetschen

Galerie Neue Meister,
Dresden, Gal. no. 2197 E

LITERATURE
Börsch-Supan/Jähnig 1973,
p.313, no. 188. Dresden 1987,
p.140, no. 390.

There are currently fourteen paintings by Caspar David Friedrich in the collections of the Galerie Neue Meister in Dresden, forming the core of its holdings of works by the Romantics. Friedrich can be regarded as the consummate master of early Romantic landscape painting. His work would have sufficed by itself to form our notion of Romantic painting. The symbolic language of his landscapes derives its vocabulary from the study of nature, and is based on a meditative internalisation of the experiences of the senses.

The work exhibited here was purchased for the Gemäldegalerie from Schloss Tetschen in 1921, together with the *Cross in the Mountains* (Galerie Neue Meister, Gal. no. 2197 D). A work of identical size showing the same region, although at dusk, found its way at the same time to Stuttgart. In the *Bohemian Landscape with Mount Milleschauer* Friedrich focuses more poignantly than otherwise on human life in the here and now.

The painting conveys his impressions of the countryside in the Bohemian mountains south of Teplitz. Our gaze is taken to the right to Mount Milleschauer, and then, because of the painting's symmetrical structure, to the equally sweeping profile of a second mountain, the Kletschen, to the left. The eye returns from the bluish-green silhouette of these distant mountains to the luscious green sloping pastures at the front. From there it travels down the path to the low-built house in the valley lying, half-concealed, amidst the trees and bushes; the presence of human life is revealed by the column of smoke rising from its chimney. Or we may climb in our minds up the hill to the right of the house, which becomes an increasingly pale yellowish-green with height, perhaps to gain an even better perspective of the landscape. The ease with which the beginning of this path in the foreground takes us on a tour of the scene seems to correspond with the tranquil state of mind brought about by the painting, and accords perfectly with its depiction of nature. With its wonderful delicacy and its relaxed, serene mood, the painting must be one of the most beautiful landscapes in German art. GS

16
Johan Christian Dahl (Bergen 1788 – Dresden 1857)
View of Dresden at Full Moon, 1839

Signed lower centre:
JDahl 1839

Oil on canvas,
78 × 130 cm

1937 from the Berlin art
market, purchased with
the help of the Dresdener
Museumsverein

Galerie Neue Meister,
Dresden, Gal. no. 2206 D

LITERATURE
Bang 1987, no. 886. Dresden
1987, p. 122, no. 250.

Dahl came from Bergen in Norway. He visited Dresden in 1818 at the end of his student days in Copenhagen as part of a lengthier tour, which ended with him taking up residence in the city on the Elbe. He became the second great master of the Romantic landscape movement in Dresden beside Caspar David Friedrich. Dahl's nocturnal panorama of the famous buildings on the Elbe captures the unique atmosphere of Dresden, the artistic and royal capital, in a most striking manner. This painting, which numbers among Dahl's most famous works, must be seen as a homage to the *genius loci* of the city he had adopted many years earlier.

Silvery moonlight gives the row of magnificent Baroque buildings of the old town, viewed here from the far shore, an unworldly air. Their glittering splendour is eclipsed by the poetic atmosphere and supplanted by the fascination exerted by the location itself. Certain motifs in this city view recall the paintings of Caspar David Friedrich, with whom Dahl shared a house, 33 An der Elbe, from 1823. But Dahl was less concerned with expressing symbolic content than with faithfully recording a marvellous view of the city, taken from almost exactly the same spot as Bellotto's famous *Dresden from the Right Bank of the Elbe, Below the Augustusbrücke* (cat. 31) almost one hundred years before. Above the broad arches of the bridge, which is teeming with people, we can discern the buildings on the Brühlsche Terrasse: first of all to the left the former Gemäldegalerie, the location for the annual exhibitions of the Dresden Academy where Dahl's paintings had been exhibited with great success since 1819. This is followed by the former Brühlsche Bibliothek that in 1719 came to house the Königlich Sächsischen Kunstakademie, which elected Dahl to no more than associate professor in 1824. Rising behind in all its power and elegance is the dome of the Frauenkirche, the crowning point of Dresden's skyline. To the right we see first of all the distant tower of the Kreuzkirche am Altmarkt, followed by the Catholic Hofkirche and, rising behind its nave into the night sky, the Hausmannsturm of the royal residence. The silhouettes of these buildings are mirrored in the surface of the river, so that the reflection of the warm lights from the windows by the river intensifies the feeling of magic that envelops the scene. The figures on the near shore, seen performing their everyday activities, harmonise with the mood of the ending day. Last chores are being brought to an end, evening fires are already aglow, a horse and horseman seek refreshment in the waters of the river; from this vantage point, the hustle and bustle on the bridge disappears into the background. GS

The
Italian
School

17

Andrea Mantegna (Isola di Cartura, near Padua 1431 – Mantua 1506)

The Holy Family, *c.* 1495–1500

Oil on canvas,
75 × 61.5 cm

1876, from the estate
of Sir Charles Eastlake,
London

Gal. no. 51

LITERATURE
Tietze-Conrat 1955, p. 181.
Bellonci and Garavaglia
1967, p. 116, no. 84.
Camesasca 1992, pp. 68ff.
Dresden 1992, p. 256.
Hamburg 2002, p. 49, no. 13.

Andrea Mantegna's *Holy Family* does not number among the works acquired by Augustus the Strong and his son Augustus III, who were chiefly interested in the High Renaissance and the Baroque. Major works from the earlier Italian schools only came to be included in the Gemäldegalerie after 1850, when developments in contemporary art – such as the Nazarenes and the Pre-Raphaelites – turned general attention to art predating 1500. In addition, King John of Saxony, the translator of Dante's *Divine Comedy*, encouraged the Gemäldegalerie to make these late purchases. They include works by Antonello da Messina, Piero di Cosimo, Botticelli, Lorenzo Costa and Lorenzo di Credi, as well as Mantegna's masterpiece, *The Holy Family*, which was acquired as late as 1876 from the estate of Sir Charles Eastlake in London.

The composition of the painting is clearly reminiscent of Antique reliefs, which use the same strict arrangement of figures in a row, with the heads all on the same level. The body of the Infant Christ standing on the lap of the Mother of God stands out with great plasticity from the dark background. The stern faces on the edge of the picture, Joseph to the left and Elizabeth to the right, resemble realistic Roman character busts, while Mary and the child show in their gracefulness a kinship to the Florentine reliefs of the early Renaissance, such as those by Luca della Robbia. The young John the Baptist in the lower right corner is shown with his mouth open, as if in speech, and pointing up at Jesus. His gaze directed at the viewer, his gesture, and the banderole with the legend 'Ecce Agnus Dei' (Behold the Lamb of God) all point to his role as the forerunner of Jesus. The twig in the form of the cross can be seen as a symbol of Christ's later crucifixion, by which he takes away the sins of the world, according to the next lines of the Agnus Dei.

Since its restoration two years ago at the J. Paul Getty Museum in Los Angeles by Christoph Schölzel, the viewer can now again behold the artist's sensitive and finely differentiated use of colour. During the restoration it was discovered that the composition was originally appreciably narrower to the left and right, much as in a very similar painting by Mantegna at the Museo di Castelvecchio in Verona. Areas of canvas were left unpainted on the two sides, and an unknown painter later added the missing parts, mostly sections of the robes. No effort was made to remove these additions during restoration or to conceal them behind an inset inside a decorative frame. The dimensions of Mantegna's original composition can still be seen, however, particularly since the missing portions of the haloes have not been added at the perimeter.

The reminiscences of Antiquity in this painting show once again Mantegna's importance for the development of the art of the High Renaissance. The majority of commentators regard this as a late work and date it to the end of the fifteenth century. GJMW

18
Titian, actually Tiziano Vecellio (Pieve di Cadore, Dolomites 1476 or *c.* 1485/90 – 1576 Venice)
Portrait of a Man with a Palm, 1561

Inscribed lower left:
M.D.LXI / ANNO [...]
NATVS / AETATIS SVAE
XLVI / TITIANVS PICTOR
ET / AEQVES CAESARIS

Oil on canvas, 138 × 116 cm

First mentioned in the
Guarienti inventory 1747–50,
no. 432, from the Casa
Marcello in Venice

Gal. no. 172

LITERATURE
Wethey 1971, no. 69.
Dresden 1992, p.386. Paris
1993, pp.614ff., no. 254.
Warsaw 1997, p.91.
Pedrocco 2000, p.266, no.
226. Hamburg 2002, pp.52ff.,
no. 15.

NOTE
1 'fù della casa Marcelli
  Nobili Veneti'.

In his Dresden inventory of 1747–50, which was never to develop beyond a fragment, Pietro Guarienti describes the origin of this painting as: 'from the noble Venetian family Marcello'.[1] Whether the sitter is a member of the Marcello family remains beyond our knowledge. On its purchase, the painting was thought to depict Pietro Aretino as a result of a forged inscription; a portrait of the renowned poet and friend of Titian would doubtless have constituted a more interesting buy than a picture of some little-known Venetian civil servant or entrepreneur. The remains of the original inscription, uncovered between 1867 and 1877, cast no more light on the sitter's identity. In 1905, H. Cook suggested that the painting depicted the painter Antonio Palma, the nephew of Palma Vecchio and father of Palma Giovane, proposing that the object by the window was a paint box and that the palm was a visual translation of the surname. But it would be rare and somewhat curious for a name to be included in this fashion by an attribute; the palm may equally be a mark of distinction, whether as a sign of martyrdom (some writers have claimed they can see a halo about the sitter) or of membership of a brotherhood. For a variety of reasons, all attempts to identify the person have remained purely speculative.

Titian presents his sitter in an imposing manner as a dignitary whose face, with its penetrating gaze, does not to betray a flicker of emotion. The severity of the presentation is given a surprisingly lyrical counterweight in the form of the evening landscape to the left. The artist has worked here with open, more diffuse brush strokes, which in places allow the grey ground to show through. Titian was to make extensive use of this method in his late work, even to the extent of applying paint with his fingers. GJMW

19

Paolo Caliari, known as Veronese (Verona 1528 – Venice 1588)
The Resurrection of Christ, c. 1570

Oil on canvas, 136 × 104 cm

Acquired 1741 by Gallery Superintendent Riedel in Vienna. According to the Dresden inventory by Pietro Guarienti 1747–50, no. 334, from Prague

Gal. no. 235

LITERATURE
Pignatti 1976, pp. 137ff., no. 184. Cocke, in London 1983, pp. 239ff., no. 143. Walther, in Essen 1986, pp. 345ff., no. 460. Weber, in Warsaw 1997, p. 92, no. II, 40.

Veronese's magnificently sumptuous paintings underwent a reappraisal during the first half of the eighteenth century when Venetian artists such as Sebastiano Ricci and Giambattista Tiepolo began to emulate him some 150 years after his death. It is not surprising that Augustus III in Dresden acquired a significant number of Veronese's works at that time, including – with a report by Tiepolo – a large-format depiction of the *The Rape of Europa* (now attributed to his workshop), and the imposing cycle of four large works in horizontal format that Veronese painted around 1571 for the Venetian Cuccina family.

The work on view here, which is exceptionally well preserved, is in a relatively small format, but is all the more brilliant for that. Its subject is the resurrection of Christ, which occurred in a miraculous manner, despite the sealed tomb and the presence of guards watching over it, on the third day after his crucifixion (Matthew XXVII, 57 – XXVIII, 7). The Saviour, who bears the stigmata of the Passion, floats upwards from the tomb with outstretched arms and his gaze directed heavenwards. Veronese visualises the miracle by means of the fiercely gesticulating soldiers, who respond with signs of fear and horror. In the background to the right the artist depicts a later scene, with a repetition of the tomb: the arrival of the women in the morning to anoint Christ's body. They found the sepulchre empty; an angel was there to tell them what had occurred on that first Easter Day.

Veronese took as his guide an altarpiece by Titian dating from 1522 (SS. Nazaro e Celso, Brescia). The Titian largely dictated the asymmetry in Veronese's painting, but he increased the elegance and tightness of his composition by including a number of overlaps between the different spatial layers and figures, and by the addition of the ruins on the left. Moreover, the great variety in colours gives the impression that Veronese was intent here on creating a real *pièce de resistance*. GJMW

20

Annibale Carracci (Bologna 1560 – Rome 1609)

Christ Wearing the Crown of Thorns, Supported by Angels, *c. 1585/87*

Oil on canvas, 85 × 100 cm

Acquired 1746 from the Galleria Estense, Modena; first mentioned in the Guarienti inventory 1747–50, fol. 31*r*, no. 150

Gal. no. 302

LITERATURE
Malvasia 1678, vol. 1, p.386. Heineken 1753–57, vol. 1, p. 18. Voss 1924, pp.489ff. Posse 1929, p.147, no. 302. Posner 1971, vol. 1, pp.17, 41, no. 34. Dresden 1992, p.139, no. 302.

NOTES
1 To name one example, Giovanni Bellini's St Vincent Ferrer altarpiece in SS. Giovanni e Paolo, Venice.
2 Malvasia 1678, vol. 1, p.386.

Christ, shown at the centre of this work as a half-length figure supported by two angels, dominates the picture. His naked upper body leans forward and slightly to the left, a movement continued by his head, which bears the crown of thorns and is surrounded by a halo. The face of the Saviour, shown in profile, streams with blood and is partly cast in shadow by the heavy crown of thorns; the eyes and mouth are half-open. Christ wears a white cloth about his loins, and a red cloak slips from his shoulders. The angel to the left is clothed in a white cape held together by a brooch and supports Christ's bent right arm with his two hands, placed one on top of the other. To the right a second angel, mouth open, looks upwards in lamentation. The light, shining flesh tones of the Saviour are lent additional intensity by their contrast with the warm, yellowish-brown of the wall behind. To the right is a narrow stretch of countryside with a tree leaning to the right, in a compositional correspondence with Christ's twisted body.

Annibale Carracci's picture of Christ is remarkable on several counts. In iconographic terms a depiction of the Ecce Homo and not, as a first impression might suggest, an angel Pietà, the picture shows Jesus still alive. Formally, however, Carracci bases his composition more on the motifs of the Man of Sorrows or the Lamentation, which show the dead Christ supported by Mary and Joseph or two angels. The early Renaissance in northern Italy, and above all in Venice, offers plenty of such examples, particularly of depictions with half-length figures.[1] Although Christ wears the crown of thorns and a purple robe, as is customary for this subject, he lacks the 'sceptre' and the fetters on his hands. Above all he is not flanked by his tormentors, but rather by two angels who support him in a gesture of mercy. Christ in his suffering is no longer presented to the Jewish people for their hatred and scorn; rather, the compassionate viewer is addressed via the angel who looks out from the picture.

The painting is one of the one hundred works that Augustus III acquired in 1746 from Modena. According to Malvasia, the picture is a work from Annibale's early period that was painted for the church of San Prospero in Reggio.[2] Posner points to Annibale's influence in connection with an Ecce Homo by Correggio in the National Gallery in London. A copy of the current painting is to be found in the Musée Magnin in Dijon, and Michael Keyl engraved it 1753 for the *Receuil d'estampes* edited by Carl Heinrich von Heineken. JG

21

Giovanni Benedetto Castiglione (Genoa 1609 – Mantua 1664)

In Front of Noah's Ark, *c.* 1650

Oil on canvas,
145 × 194.5 cm

Engraved in 1757 for
P. Aveline's *Galeriewerk*

This work and *The Return
of Jacob* were purchased
as pendants by de Brais and
Araignon in 1742 from the
Carignan Collection, Paris,
for 12,000 livres; Guarienti
inventory 1747–50, fol. 38*r*,
no. 73

Gal. no. 659

LITERATURE
Riedel and Wenzel 1765,
p. 208, no. I, 214. Delogu
1928, p. 24. Posse 1929,
pp. 321ff., nos 659, 660.
Genoa 1990, p. 133. Dijon
2001, no. 60.

NOTES
1 The Dresden
  Gemäldegalerie has
  two examples of *The
  Israelites in the Desert*
  (Gal. nos 253, 260) and
  two of *Noah's Ark*
  (Gal. nos 258A, 261).

When studying in Genoa under Giovanni Battista Paggi (documented in 1626–27), Castiglione was in contact with the colony of northern artists in the city, above all with the Flemings Lucas and Cornelis de Wael, as well as with Anthony van Dyck. From these painters Castiglione developed a realistic style of great immediacy, concentrating above all on animals and still-lifes set mostly in landscapes with religious staffage. Already in 1635 he was named in a document as a specialist for patriarchal processions, and for scenes from the Old Testament showing the wanderings of the Israelites. The Gemäldegalerie Alte Meister in Dresden has two such pictures, both showing *The Return of Jacob*, the larger of which is illustrated here (p. 79).

The Bible tells us of the difficulties experienced by Jacob, Isaac's chosen son, in taking a wife while staying abroad with his uncle, Laban. Jacob loved Rachel, and worked for Laban for seven years in order to marry her, only to be given instead her older sister Leah; he was told he would have to work another seven years to receive Rachel. His wages were to be the speckled and spotted cattle from Laban's herd, but Jacob realised that Laban had picked these out and led them off for himself. Jacob hit on the ruse of breeding strong animals with such markings, so that finally he had 'much cattle, and maidservants, and menservants, and camels, and asses'; with these he flew from Canaan (Genesis XXX, 43; XXXI, 17–21). Castiglione shows Jacob's return in two zones: large in the foreground on a dark wedge-shaped section of the landscape, paler and smaller in the middleground. In neither case is the beginning or the end of his train visible, thus suggesting an enormous company. While in the foreground kitchen utensils are still being gathered together, the company in the background is already underway. The two groups maintain eye contact; Jacob's family is in the upper right of the foreground. Presumably he is the only figure who looks out from the painting.

The painting exhibited takes us back to even more ancient times. Before the Flood, Noah was charged by God to build an ark and to save a male and a female of every species (Genesis VII, 1–9). Once again, Castiglione skilfully depicts only part of the event and part of the wooden ship, so that the immensity of its size and the enormity of the number of animals is left to the viewer's imagination. Noah arranges the entry of the animals, which have assembled in two lines parallel to the picture plane. Curiously they consist only of European indigenous animals, many of them domestic.

The subject of Noah's ark can already be seen in Castiglione's work from the early 1630s, in a large painting at the Accademia Ligustica di Belle Arti, Genoa, and in another at the Uffizi, Florence. Later, in his riper years between 1645 and 1655, Castiglione produced versions that are closer to the painting in Dresden, including one in Nantes at the Musée des Beaux-Arts that closely matches a 1654 work owned privately in Genoa. This gives us a starting point for the dating of the Dresden picture. Whether or not the two paintings were planned by Castiglione as pendants, it is clear that they were not composed symmetrically; besides, *In Front of Noah's Ark* uses a more intensive palette. Consequently, *The Return of Jacob* has been dated to the 1630s.

In Italy, such subjects had already been treated in a similar manner by Jacopo Bassano, who also painted dense convoys of people and animals in the lower halves

of his pictures so that they resemble the pattern of a carpet.[1] His palette, however, was much darker, with only the occasional patch of local colour flashing out from a ground painted in dark browns and black. Castiglione dazzles with a strong but well-considered tonality before a sky in reds and blues, applying paint thickly to produce a tactile quality and forcing contrasting greens and reds, yellows and blues into tight clusters – as in the kitchen utensils, say, or the eyes of the cat in *In Front of Noah's Ark* – thus conveying the substance of the objects in a highly convincing way. In this his work touches on the Flemish style of Frans Snyder or Jan Fyt (it was not by chance that Pieter Boel, a pupil of Fyt, was to do his apprenticeship under Castiglione). *In Front of Noah's Ark* and *The Return of Jacob* are great testimonies to the work of an artist, not merely as a painter but even more so as a draughtsman, who ranks among the most outstanding of the seventeenth century. This was reflected when the Dresden Gemäldegalerie was set up in 1754, for the two paintings were hung among the choicest pieces on either side of Correggio's *Holy Night*. GJMW

The Return of Jacob,
c. 1630/40. Oil on canvas,
144 x 198 cm. Gal. no. 660

Giuseppe Maria Crespi (Bologna 1665 – Bologna 1747)

Baptism, 1712
Confession, c.1712

Baptism, 1712
Inscribed left on the font:
MDCCXII; and on the rim
of the font: FONS VI ...

Oil on canvas,
127 × 95 cm

Confession, c. 1712
Inscribed on the roof
of the confessional: UT
JUSTIFICERIS; on the
notice inside: CASVS
RESERV[...]

Oil on canvas,
127 × 94.5 cm

Etched by Johann Anton
Riedel (1754), engraved
by Lorenzo Zucchi

Both paintings were
acquired in around 1744
from the estate of Cardinal
Ottoboni, Rome; Guarienti
inventory 1747–50, fol. 24r,
nos 94, 92

Gal. nos 396, 398

LITERATURE
Posse 1929, pp.178ff.
Merriman 1980, pp.317ff.,
nos 290, 293. Fort Worth
1986, pp.132ff. Vienna 1988,
pp.32ff., nos 4, 7. Bologna
1990, pp.86ff., 336ff., no. 45.
Columbus 1999, pp. 207ff.,
no. 5.

NOTES
1 Zanotti 1739, vol. 2,
  pp.53ff.
2 Crespi 1769, pp.212ff.
3 Our thanks to Dr Wilhelm
  Hollstein, Münzkabinett
  Dresden.

Confirmation, c. 1712.
Oil on canvas, 125.5 x 93 cm.
Gal. no. 395

Communion, c. 1712.
Oil on canvas, 127.5 x 94.5 cm.
Gal. no. 397

These two paintings belong to a series by Crespi depicting the seven sacraments as individual scenes: baptism, confession, confirmation, communion, extreme unction, ordination and matrimony. In 1739, while Crespi was still alive, the Bolognese Gianpietro Zanotti gave a thorough account of the origin of the paintings: 'One day Crespi saw a man in the confessional at San Benedetto's confessing his sins to the priest. A ray of sunlight fell on the man's head and shoulders, and was reflected inside the small chamber to produce the most beautiful contrast between light and dark that can be imagined. He [Crespi] studied it very carefully and, as soon as he was back home, did a small drawing of the scene. Then he sent two porters to fetch him a confessional, which he promptly installed in his room with staged lighting. He introduced Ludovico Mattioli, who chanced to be there, into the scene of the confession, and painted him so well that everyone recognised him, as they did the priest, who was the same person who had lent him the confessional.'[1] Zanotti further recounts that Crespi made a gift of the painting to Cardinal Pietro Ottoboni in Rome, who was highly delighted and commissioned the remaining six paintings.

Whether or not the *Confession* came about in the way described, Zanotti uses certain phrases to praise the artist that are aimed at drawing attention to a central aspect of the paintings: the astonishing realism with which a holy sacrament is depicted as a scene from everyday life. In complete contrast, Nicolas Poussin had painted two series of the seven sacraments in Rome in the mode of academic history painting, using precious local colours and invoking classical antiquity in the way he painted the robes. Consequently Crespi's paintings had to be shown by anecdotal means to have originated in a 'real' occurrence, and even be made out to be comical. Zanotti explains that Crespi deliberately chose humorous topics, such that 'there was much laughter at the representation and the idea' of this confession. Similarly the writer detected amusing details in the matrimony painting: the groom was around 80, the bride just 14; and the two witnesses in the background appeared to be taking snuff and pouring scorn on this unequal marriage. Luigi Crespi, the son of the painter, further adorned Zanotti's tales in 1769 when he noted the hot wax dripping onto the hand of a monk in the extreme unction picture, and drew attention to the stoop of the bishop in the confirmation scene as he touches the child before him.[2]

Extreme Unction, *c.* 1712.
Oil on canvas, 127 x 94.5 cm.
Gal. no. 394

Ordination, *c.* 1712.
Oil on canvas, 127 x 95 cm.
Gal. no. 393

Matrimony, *c.* 1712.
Oil on canvas, 127 x 93.5 cm.
Gal. no. 392

Humour also strongly informs the confession: the painting begins as a depiction of a simple, coarsely constructed confessional; beneath its door's ornamental curves the rounded toes of the priest's less than elegant shoes can be seen. Well-fed and bald-headed, the priest gives a blessing; we can only conjecture to whom, although the snatch of clothing that is visible suggests a woman. He will shortly turn to the remorseful sinner on the other side, whose bald pate has been caught just as effectively by a sunbeam as the priest's. The printed note inside the confessional for a special 'casus' points to a number of incongruities, as does the large inscription above, which correctly should read 'ut iustifaceris' (that you have acted justly).[3]

The representation of the baptism likewise contains several oddities: the priest ladles the water of the 'Source of Life' (according to the inscription) over the infant. The child's father holds it somewhat clumsily over the font, while the elegant mother merely places a hand on the child's back. Whispering is going on behind the couple; a person on the extreme right points at the scene, while another calls for silence by placing his finger to his lips. Doubtless Crespi deliberately placed the head between the married couple and made the gesture ambiguous to raise doubts about the relationship between the two parents, and questions of paternity.

Crespi treats the subjects of his paintings realistically, while simultaneously making much of incidental matters that distract from the main action, matters which belong more to chance occurrences in a genuine religious scene and not to an idealised one. Unlike Poussin, who illustrated the sacrament of baptism with Christ's baptism by John, Crespi sites the sacrament in the everyday world and thus the field of genre painting. His scenes take place in the lower strata of society, among simple people with all their faults. Elevated to the religious sphere of the seven sacraments, they can appear incongruous, both in a painting as well as on the stage. Indeed, parallels with comedy are hard to overlook, for here as there the scenes are filled with ill-suited loving couples, intrigues, mutterings and whispers. In some ways this also extends to Crespi's choice of colours and painting technique: much as the characters in popular romps speak a coarse and simple language, Crespi paints his series in a crude and simple manner, albeit with all the bravura of the experienced painter.

The smirks of Zanotti and Luigi Crespi become quite understandable when we see the results of reflecting a sublime subject in the comical mirror of genre painting. The delights of this anti-academic approach will not have been wasted on the series's first owner, Cardinal Ottoboni, a champion of Classicist painting in Rome, as practised by Francesco Trevisani and Sebastiano Conca.

Crespi dated the *Baptism* to 1712, giving us a clue to the dating of the whole series. A large number of replicas and copies, such as the drawn and engraved versions that Pierre-Charles Trémolières made in 1734, speaks for the popularity of these paintings. Pietro Longhi also made a series of the seven sacraments as genre paintings; similar in content, they differ from Crespi's in formal terms. GJMW

Canaletto, actually Antonio Canal (Venice 1697 – Venice 1768)

The Grand Canal, Venice, Looking North from Near the Rialto Bridge, *c.* 1726
The Grand Canal, Venice, Looking from Palazzo Balbi, *c.* 1726

Oil on canvas,
149.5 × 197 cm

Oil on canvas,
148 × 196 cm

Both first in the 1754
Dresden inventory, I, 524,
525 (store)

Inv. no. 52/20
Inv. no. 52/105

LITERATURE
Constable 1962, no. 211;
no. 231. Constable/Links
1989, no. 211; no. 231.
Dresden 1992, p. 138.
Venice 2001B, pp. 114, 126.

NOTES
1 Columbus 1999, pp. 200ff.;
   Venice 2001B, pp. 126ff.
2 Venice 2001B, p. 148.

These two large-format *vedute* were first listed in the Dresden inventory of 1754, interestingly in a separate section reserved for paintings in the store. This was remarkable because the section almost exclusively contained modern, and above all Venetian, paintings, including five more *vedute* of Venice by Canaletto, one by Luca Carlevaris, as well as all the views of Verona, Dresden and Pirna that Bernardo Bellotto, Canaletto's nephew, had painted up until then. It is apparent that no decision had been made as to where to display this large collection of new works. The list is all the more interesting in that the five other works by Canaletto and the painting by Carlevaris had certainly been painted for the Imperial Ambassador in Venice, Count Giambattista Colloredo (1656–1729), who had celebrated his installation in the Doge's Palace – the subject of Carlevaris's painting – on 3 April 1726. Since the two *vedute* on view here can be dated on the strength of their style to the same year, it seems likely that they were also painted for Colloredo, and later purchased along with his other paintings. Their format speaks in favour of a royal client, although in that case this could equally have been Elector Friedrich Augustus I.[1] But it was not until after the Second World War that the two paintings finally came to the Gemäldegalerie; prior to that they had been used to adorn palaces and castles, last of all Schloss Pillnitz. This is also the reason why they are not to be found in any of the Gemäldegalerie's older catalogues.

The relationship of the two large *vedute* to Canaletto's production from around 1725 is further clarified by the fact that the artist also painted the same views for other clients, one in 1723 for Joseph Wenzel Liechtenstein, and the other in 1725 for Stefano Conti. Four paintings in the same format as the two at Dresden were received by the Prince of Liechtenstein. Similarly, Stefano Conti of Lucca ordered four views in 1725/26; Canaletto's contracts, descriptions and receipts for them have all survived. Among these works for Conti is the same view with the Fabbriche Nuove found in Dresden, although on a more modest scale. In his receipt for payment on 25 November 1725, Canaletto stresses that the paintings are to be viewed as a group together.[2] Even if the subject of the Conti pendant differs from that in Dresden, the two works exhibited here complement each other on account of their mutual subject, the Grand Canal, their compositions, which in both cases have the vanishing point at the centre, and their lighting. The heavy shadow to the right or left rounds off the two paintings on their outer edges.

In Canaletto's day, the only crossing that spanned the largest waterway in Venice was the imposing Rialto Bridge, which consequently became the hub of both business life and traffic and a point of orientation amid the confusion of Venice's smaller canals and alleys. The artist shows the bridge in the *veduta* that looks out to the north-east from Palazzo Balbi, while in the other we have already passed it and are looking further to the north. Even today we can see a corner of the open vegetable market there on the left, with beside it – cast in shadow in the painting – the Fabbriche Nuove di Rialto, and behind that the fish market and the tall Palazzo Pesaro. Opposite we see to the right the Palazzi Michiel del Brusa and Michiel dalle Colonne, and behind them the gondola landing stage at the Ca' d'Oro.

In the pendant, Canaletto shows on the far left a section of the Palazzo Balbi, to the right the Palazzo Contarini dalle Figure and the four palazzi of the Mocenigo family. In the distance we can see the Rialto Bridge, and beyond that to the right the

roof of the church of SS. Giovanni e Paolo. In none of his other *vedute* has Canaletto placed such a curiously manned gondola in the foreground: the vessel, decorated with green twigs, contains two figures in Commedia dell'Arte costumes who seem to have escaped from the stage. The gondola, readied for a delightful picnic trip, is the scene of a marital drama, for the ugly old woman is clearly beating the man over his pointed hat with her oar, as he holds a tightly bundled infant out to her imploringly. This scene has yet to be identified in a play or comedy.

Canaletto's cityscapes are not simply topographical studies; they are artistically composed works with their own consciously created atmospheres and *mises en scène*. A panoply of colours are cast from the heaving skies onto the interlocking buildings and the surface of the water. All manner of gondolas enliven the waters, while the people at the windows, on the balconies or on the boats add further splashes of colour to the scene. GJMW

26

Giovanni Battista Piazzetta (Treviso 1682 – Venice 1754)

A Young Ensign, c.1742

Oil on canvas,
87 × 71.5 cm

Engraved by Lorenzo
Zucchi

Acquired 1743 from Count
Francesco Algarotti in
Venice; first in
Riedel/Wenzel 1765,
G.E. no. 677

Gal. no. 571

LITERATURE
Posse 1929, p.272. Dresden
1968, pp.81ff., no. 78. Venice
1969, p.130, no. 55. Mariusz
1982, no. 87. Essen 1986, no.
465. Knox 1992, pp.197ff., fig.
142. Columbus 1999, no. 66.

NOTES
1 Aragon and Cocteau 1957.
2 Mariusz 1982, no. 86.
3 'le plus élaboré et le plus
studieux de tous';
'extrèmement long, et très
difficile à gouverner'.
4 'qui me mène de mois en
mois sans rien conclurre.
Je m'en vais venir aux
plus fortes demarches…'
Posse 1931, p.51, 67.
5 Inv. Dresden 1754, I, 551;
since 1755 in Schloss
Hubertusburg, no. 3819;
auctioned Amsterdam 22
May 1765, no. 57. Weber
1996, pp.181ff., 189.

A youth leans against a battered pedestal, casually supporting himself on his left arm; his right hand grasps the pole of a white flag, which falls in gentle folds onto his shoulder. The motifs in this picture can be quickly enumerated, but the quality of the painting itself is incomparably rich. The deep blue of the young man's jacket is broken by the turquoise lining of his collar, which mediates the gold tones of the brocade below. The white flag visits every nuance of cold and warm in shades of grey and ochre; the fabric reflects the light, is permeated by the light, tempers it and consigns it back into the shadows. The white creates a tense backdrop to the face shown in profile; an enormous range of contrasts from the brightest shades to the darkness of the background is manifested in a rich web of juxtapositions.

The imagery of the painting is reminiscent in its central motif – a figure leaning on a pedestal – of portraiture, while the pathos of the flag and the young man's attentive gaze are more reminiscent of historical painting. 'This youngster is a cousin of Gavroche on the barricades. Delacroix and Courbet would have placed him in one of their scenes of the Paris Commune,' as Jean Cocteau said of him in conversation with Louis Aragon, adding: 'He remains on the brink of a possible event. It is clear that if it started he would rush into the fray with a passion, holding up his flag in a hail of bullets. But he could equally take part, quite unchanged, in a Corpus Christi procession.'[1] This, then, is a genre painting, but of the order of a historical painting, albeit without any definite theme – 'L'Enseigne en Idée' is the title that Zucchi gave his subsequent engraving – and thus it is open to many associations.

The painting's point of departure lies in the painterly effects offered by chiaroscuro. Rembrandt had already worked in a similar way to paint and etch picturesque figures in fantastic costumes, equipped as warlike or Oriental potentates with swords and flags; Zanetti, for example, had a complete set of Rembrandt's etchings at the time in Venice. Piazzetta painted and drew a number of similarly indeterminate figures, partly in a genre or pastoral scene, partly militaristic with the figure dressed as a standard-bearer, archer or lancer. The Dresden painting comes particularly close to the depiction of a young pilgrim painted in 1738/39 using the same model (Art Institute of Chicago). Knox considers the subject to be the painter's own son, Giacomo, born in 1725, which would give further credence to dating the painting to 1742.[2]

Count Francesco Algarotti was intent on awakening an enthusiasm in Augustus III for contemporary Venetian painting, and called for modern works to be included in the growing collections in Dresden. To further this strategy he purchased two brand new paintings by Piazzetta in 1743: the *Young Ensign* and the *David with the Head of Goliath* (Gal. no. 570). He also commissioned a series of six paintings by Venetian artists, including one by Piazzetta. Although in a letter of 9 August 1743 he describes the painter as 'the most sophisticated and studious of all', Algarotti also characterises him as 'a slow worker, and very difficult to control'.[3] In September 1745 he still complains that Piazzetta has 'led me on for months and months with no conclusion. I shall have to take stronger measures…'.[4] It is thus all the more regrettable that Piazzetta's *Caesar and the Pirates of Cilicia*, which was delivered in 1746 to Dresden, has not been discovered since it was auctioned in 1765 in Amsterdam.[5] GJMW

27

Giuseppe Nogari (Venice 1699 – Venice 1763)
Peter the Apostle, 1743

Inscribed on the reverse:
Joseph Nogari / Venetus
pinxit / 1743

Oil on canvas,
84.5 × 60.5 cm

Purchased in 1743 by
Algarotti from the painter
in Venice; first in the
Guarienti inventory of
1747–50, fol. 42r, no. 231

Gal. no. 593

LITERATURE
Posse 1929, p. 284. Vienna
1988, no. 26. Weber and
Henning 1998, pp. 46ff.,
no. 15.

Giuseppe Nogari's works were bought by Augustus III during his own lifetime. Count Francesco Algarotti suggested these contemporary acquisitions, and set about the task in 1743 in Venice, at the same time purchasing Piazzetta's *Young Ensign* (cat. 27). That same year saw not only *Peter the Apostle* being sent to Dresden, but also four profane personifications by Nogari, in which the artist – in keeping with fashion – had undertaken a personal reappraisal of the work of Rembrandt from one hundred years earlier (Gal. nos 589, 590, 591 [lost in 1945] and 592).

Nogari lived his whole life in Venice and in 1756 became a member of the Accademia di Pittura e Scultura. From the 1730s he became widely known among collectors north of the Alps for his allegorical and religious portraits done as half-length and head studies. He also painted a number of altarpieces in his native city.

The present work shows Peter as the bringer of God's word. His right hand points to the Bible, while his gaze is directed in the diametrically opposite direction to the light entering from the upper left, which embodies the source of divine inspiration. Peter, himself the author of two epistles to the Hebrew community, is fully aware that the text is not his own work: '…by them that have preached the gospel unto you with the Holy Ghost sent down from heaven' (1 Peter I, 12). The apostle holds a key of bronze and one of gold, thus underlining his authority as the 'rock' upon which Christ will build his church (Matthew XVI, 18). Christ entrusted the keys to Peter, saying, 'Whatsoever thou shalt bind on earth shall be bound in heaven; and whatsoever thou shalt loose on earth shall be loosed in heaven' (Matthew XVI, 19).

In keeping with Christ's prophecy (John XXI, 18b) Peter died a martyr's death at a great age. Nogari emphasises the apostle's age in his picture, skilfully revealing his elderly body. Peter's right shoulder, his face, worked in thick paint, and his wispy grey hair are placed most fully in the light and stand out boldly from the dark, diffuse background. AH

28

Bernardo Bellotto, known as Canaletto (Venice 1722 – Warsaw 1780)

Dresden from the Right Bank of the Elbe, Above the Augustusbrücke, 1747

Signed lower right on the block of stone: BERNARDO. BELOTTO / DETTO CANALETO / F.ANNO 1747. IN. DRESDA

Oil on canvas, 132 × 236 cm

First mentioned in the inventory of 1754, store, no. 543: 'Prospect of Dresden, the bridge, Elbe and the garden of the Prime Minister, Count Brühl, on canvas 4.8. 8.4.'

Gal. no. 602

LITERATURE
Dresden Cat. 1843, no. 41. Posse 1929, p.288. Fritzsche 1936. pp.13ff., 38, 51, 53, 108ff., 170, no. VG 50. Lippold 1963, p.26. Kozakiewicz 1972, vol. 1, p.84ff., 100ff., 107; vol. 2, p.107, no. 140. Camesasca 1974, no. 74. Löffler 1985, figs 1–8. Dresden 1992, p.110. Walther 1995, p.23ff. Rizzi 1996, pp. 28ff., no. 1. Warsaw 1997, p. 75. Löffler 2000, figs 1–8. Venice 2001A, p.148, no. 39. Hamburg 2002, no. 10.

Until now, the literature has failed to identify correctly the painting with the entry in the Gemäldegalerie inventory of 1754. Although it may surprise us when we read there that the subject of this painting is the Prime Minister's garden, Bellotto had himself written beneath his etching of this 1747 *veduta*: 'Perspective de la galerie, et du Jardin de son Excellence Mgr. / Le Comte de Brühl Premier Ministre…' He also mentions that the view was taken from the house of Consigliere Hoffmann, husband of the Venetian miniaturist Felicitas Sartori.

The view of the city on the distant bank of the Elbe shows a row of palaces and churches, ending at the right with the Augustusbrücke designed by Matthäus Daniel Pöppelmann. The dome of George Bähr's Frauenkirche to the far left towers above Count Brühl's Gemäldegalerie, which was situated on the old Venus bastion – the garden now known as the Brühl Terrace – beside the library, the Gartensaal and the Palais Brühl. These are then followed by the Fürstenbergsche Palais, the Georgenbau of the Castle, and the Catholic Hofkirche with its unfinished tower.

This painting is considered to be Bellotto's first view of Dresden. His signature to the lower right is conspicuous and gives not only his full name and the date 1747 but also – the sole instance among his Saxon *vedute* – the location: 'in Dresden'. Clearly he felt he should document here an important moment in his personal history, the beginning of a new phase of work prompted by his admission to an important court. The group of figures that Bellotto has placed at the middle of the picture's lower edge has a similar function: sitting at the centre before the city backdrop is a draughtsman who can only be Bellotto himself. His presence illustrates the details of his signature, thus giving double proof of the truthfulness of the *veduta*.

An older man in a green coat points out the painting's subject to Bellotto, while a second man with a round, reddened head stands behind him to the left. No historical sources exist to help us identify these and the figures further to the right, but tradition has it in the Gemäldegalerie that the more corpulent figure is the court painter Christian Wilhelm Ernst Dietrich, who was simultaneously inspector of the Königliche Gemäldegalerie, and that the older man is Johann Alexander Thiele, Bellotto's predecessor as *vedutista* at the court of Dresden. The gentlemen further to the right have been identified as the royal physician Filippo di Violante, the corpulent countertenor Niccolò Pozzi (known as Niccolini), one of the court Turks, and – standing slightly apart – the court-jester Fröhlich. Only the last can be definitively identified, for he is known from contemporary illustrations that show him wearing the costume of the Salzkammergut region of Austria.

The painting has a pendant, assuredly the most famous view of Dresden, which is taken from the same side of the Elbe but from a point further downstream, below the Augustusbrücke. That composition, dating from 1748, more or less mirrors the work on view here so that the diagonal course of the river in the two pictures is symmetrically arranged. GJMW

29

Bernardo Bellotto, known as Canaletto (Venice 1722 – Warsaw 1780)

Dresden from the Left Bank of the Elbe, Below the Fortifications, 1748

Signed front left on the
stone block: Bernardo
Bellotto Detto / Canaletto
F. An°. 1748; etched by
Bellotto with the date 1748

Oil on canvas, 135 × 238 cm

First mentioned in the
inventory of 1754, store,
no. 545: 'Prospect of the
new town near Dresden,
recorded from the Gehege,
on canvas. 4.8 8.4.'

Gal. no. 607

LITERATURE
Matthäi 1834, no. 35. Hübner
1856, no. 2176. Stübel 1923,
pp. 14ff. Posse 1929, p. 290.
Fritzsche 1936, pp. 53, 109,
no. VG 54. Lippold 1963,
p. 27, pl. 16. Kozakiewicz
1972, vol. 1, pp. 84ff., 100ff.;
vol. 2, pp. 122, 127, no. 154.
Camesasca 1974, p. 97,
no. 79. Löffler 1985, figs
21–25. Dresden 1992, p. 112.
Walther 1995, pp. 51ff., no.
14. Rizzi 1996, p. 40, no. 13.
Citati 1996, p. 44. Madrid
1998, no. 2. Columbus 1999,
no. 2. Löffler 2000, figs
21–25. Venice 2001A, p. 156,
no. 43. Hamburg 2002, no.
12.

For a long time, this *veduta* was wrongly identified with no. 539 in the inventory of 1754. The description in the correct entry, no. 545, directs our attention to the painting's real subject, the new town on the opposite shore of the Elbe. Bellotto did the same when in 1748 he entitled his etching of this view thus: 'Perspective de la ville neuve et du Palais de S. M. dit d'Hollande et des Environs de / La campagne Loschúwitz…' Consequently, the title now normally given to the painting is somewhat misleading.

Bellotto's vantage point was on the left bank of the Elbe, downriver from the city centre. He would have passed the ramparts of the old city fortifications to the right. The city moat can be seen at its beginning, where it takes in water from the Elbe, and extending to the right past the Luna Bastion and then the Zwinger, a masterpiece of festive Baroque architecture not included in this view. The rampart behind the wooden structure contained the Elector's wine cellar. The Hofkirche, still with scaffolding around its tower, forms the picture's main accent; Bellotto was later to omit the scaffolding when he etched the view. The tower that can be seen peering over the roof of the Hofkirche belongs to the dome of the Protestant Frauenkirche, located further downstream. The Augustusbrücke takes us to the far shore of the Elbe, to Dresden Neustadt, where at the end of the bridge the Blockhaus can be seen in the process of construction. Its architect, Zacharias Longuelune, had originally planned to place a stepped pyramid on top of the square building, which was to support in turn an equestrian statue of Augustus the Strong, but after Longuelune's death a plain, mezzanine storey was placed there instead. Also visible on the far left is the Japanische Palais, which emerged from the Holländische Palais built in 1715. Augustus the Strong had purchased it in 1717 and determined that it should house his collection of porcelain. The inventory of this 'small porcelain palace' of 1721 lists thousands of pieces of Chinese, Japanese and Meissen porcelain on its 884 pages. The shape of the building's roof, which was extended in the years up until 1738 into a complex with four wings, is reminiscent of Far Eastern architecture.

The view of the city occupies no more than a narrow strip of the painting; none of Bellotto's other Dresden *vedute* adheres so strongly to the horizontal. Broad stretches in the foreground are filled with incidental characters from farming life, with a cart, country folk resting and out walking, anglers and shepherds; the walls of the fortifications have been used to hang out the laundry to dry. Bellotto adopted several motifs from the Venetian landscape painter Francesco Zuccarelli, the cow shown here in the middleground among them. GJMW

30

Bernardo Bellotto, known as Canaletto (Venice 1722 – Warsaw 1780)

The Moat of the Zwinger in Dresden, between 1749 and 1753

Oil on canvas,
133 × 235 cm

Etched by Bellotto with the
date 1758

First mentioned in the
Dresden inventory of 1754,
store no. 535: 'Prospect
of Dresden, a part of the
Zwinger beside the Zwinger
Bridge, and of the avenue
to Friedrichstadt,
on canvas. 4.8 8.4'

Gal. no. 609

LITERATURE
Matthäi 1834, no. 40.
Fritzsche 1936, pp.53, 104,
110, no. VG 57. Kozakiewicz
1972, vol. 1, pp.84ff., 100ff.;
vol. 2, pp.127ff., no. 157.
Venice 1986, pp.74ff., no. 4.
London 1994, pp.372ff.,
430ff., no. 260. Venice 1995,
pp.314ff., no. 78. Walther
1995, pp.30ff., no. 5. Rizzi
1996, pp.42, no. 15. Madrid
1998, pp.114ff., no. 4.
Columbus 1999, pp.62ff.,
no. 4. Löffler 2000, figs
26–29.

Bernardo Bellotto's views of Dresden demonstrate astonishing precision both in their topographical detailing and their mastery of perspective. Such precision has frequently been attributed to the use of a camera obscura. Bellotto's paintings allow the viewer to walk around the city; the various locations of his *vedute* complement each other and forever provide new angles on already familiar sights.

This high degree of veracity can even extend to fairly unfamiliar aspects, such that sometimes confusing overlaps between individual buildings are tolerated. The subject and composition seem particularly unusual in this view. The Zwinger, one of the masterpieces of Baroque architecture, has been placed to one side where it is obscured by trees; indeed, buildings only occupy a small amount of the picture's centre, for the focus of the composition is the moat.

The old Luna Bastion of the city fortifications presents here its Scharfe Ecke, or 'sharp corner'. It was on this spot on top of the ramparts, between the castle and the moat, that Augustus the Strong had the Zwinger built between 1710 and 1732 as a festival building. The name 'Zwinger' was originally a military term – being the area between outer and inner defence walls – and had thus previously referred to the site and not to a building. Bellotto also produced a veritable portrait of the rectangular complex, constructed around its festival ground, from another viewpoint, a window of the Wallpavillon of the Zwinger just a few metres to the left (Gal. no. 629). The building's right, southern flank with the Kronentor can be seen in the centre of our picture.

To the upper left beside the trees is a corner of the Mathematisch-Physikalische Salon, built in 1712/13, which had made a home for part of the collection of the Kunstkammer. The Langgalerie of the Zwinger with the Kronentor led to the Zoologische Pavillon (1718/19), which formed a pendant to the Salon. Rising up above is a thick clump of roofs, towers and spires: the red roof belongs to Pöppelmann's Opernhaus am Zwinger, and the slate roof beyond that to the Sophienkirche. The tower of the Kreuzkirche rises to the left, while to the far left, on the painting's edge, we see the Hausmannsturm, the tower of the castle. Other imposing buildings can be seen directly above the moat, such as the brightly painted house dating from 1744 belonging to Andreas Adam, Secretary to the Department of Public Buildings, with its five large chimneys on the roof. Beside that is the squat roof of the Wilsdruffer Tor, which concealed the water tank for the fountains of the Zwinger. The half-timbered building further to the right was where the backcloths and props for the opera house were painted.

Bellotto designed the majority of his Dresden *vedute* as pairs whose subject and composition refer to one another. This painting's ascending diagonal is mirrored by a descending diagonal in the pendant (Gal. no. 611), which shows a continuation of the moat, the so-called Saturnbastei. To its extreme left the side of the Zwinger that Bellotto shows here can be seen. GJMW

31

Bernardo Bellotto, known as Canaletto (Venice 1722 – Warsaw 1780)
Dresden from the Right Bank of the Elbe, Below the Augustusbrücke, between 1751 and 1753

Oil on canvas,
95 × 165 cm

Acquired 1778 from the
estate of Chief Financial
Inspector Spahn

Gal. no. 630

LITERATURE
Posse 1929, pp. 297ff.,
no. 630. Fritzsche 1936,
pp. 53, 109, 172, no. VG 53.
Kozakiewicz 1972, vol. 2,
pp. 116ff., no. 149.
Camesasca 1974, p. 97,
no. 86. Löffler 1985, figs 9,
15. Rizzi 1996, p. 37, no. 9.
Madrid 1998, no. 1. Löffler
2000, figs 14, 15. Dijon 2001,
p. 68, no. 9. Venice 2001A,
p. 180. Hamburg 2002, no. 11.

Bellotto painted his first large view of Dresden in 1747, and complemented it a year later with a pendant. Replicas of the two pictures, painted in a smaller format but from his own hand, came to the Gemäldegalerie in 1778 from the Spahn Collection. In the present work, Bellotto has added Brühl's Belvedere (built 1749–51, destroyed 1759) to the left at the back, which was not included in the original painting of 1748, and corrected the depiction of the Brühlsche Bibliothek, the library to which in the meantime an additional storey had been added. This panorama of the city was to become the classic view of Dresden, seen approximately from the level of the Japanische Palais: the right-hand side of the painting is dominated by the Catholic Hofkirche, shining in its light shades and intensified by its reflection in the river. Although the tower had not yet been finished, Bellotto faked it on the Dresden versions of the current composition after inspecting the architect's plans. Behind the Hofkirche we see parts of the royal residence, including the lofty Hausmannsturm, which seems to rest on the roof of the Hofkirche. The Augustusbrücke as designed by Matthias Daniel Pöppelmann sweeps across the Elbe, and acts as it were as the plinth for the buildings that form the Brühlsche Terrasse behind: the palace of Anton Egon von Fürstenberg, who ruled Dresden whenever Augustus the Strong was away in Poland, followed by the Palais Brühl with its tall windows in the form of semicircular arches, and then the Brühlsche Bibliothek and the Gemäldegalerie of Count Brühl, Prime Minister to Augustus III. Rising up directly behind them is the majestic dome of the Protestant Frauenkirche, designed by George Bähr, newly built but already an integral part of Dresden's skyline.

The precision of Bellotto's *vedute* makes it easy to forget their carefully calculated compositions. The way the river forms a diagonal, or the bank in the foreground a wedge shape, or the building on the far left acts as a link between picture and frame: all accord with specific rules and conventions that developed from landscape painting. Bellotto adds a number of incidental figures, most strikingly an impoverished family at the front left who have settled outside a simple wooden hut; the arrangement of these figures is curiously reminiscent of one of the most widespread themes of religious painting, the Holy Family in the stable at Bethlehem with the adoration of the shepherds. Is it possible that Bellotto has included here a reference to the Hofkirche on the far bank of the Elbe, whose iconographic programme for the worship of the Holy Family was developed on the initiative of Queen Maria Josepha? GJMW

32

Bernardo Bellotto, known as Canaletto (Venice 1722 – Warsaw 1780)

Pirna Seen from the Harbour Town, between 1753 and 1755

Oil on canvas,
136 × 237 cm

Etched by Bellotto before
1763

Presumably delivered by the
artist before 1756; first
catalogued by Matthäi 1834,
no. 55

Gal. no. 626

LITERATURE
Matthäi 1834, no. 55.
Fritzsche 1936, pp. 54, 112,
173, no. VG 82. Kozakiewicz
1972, vol. 1, pp. 84, 100ff.;
vol. 2, p. 173, no. 217. Venice
1986, p. 91, no. 19. Walther
1995, pp. 60ff., no. 19. Rizzi
1996, p. 76, no. 54. Weber
1998A, pp. 50, 53, note 14.
Schmidt 2000, pp. 86–93.
Venice 2001A, pp. 186ff.,
no. 58.

NOTES
1 Weber 1991, pp. 130ff.
2 'Untroubled by thought,
   I only look after my flock';
   Weber 1998A, passim.

After the large *vedute* of the royal capital, Bellotto turned his attention to the smaller town of Pirna, further up the Elbe, with the royal castle of Sonnenstein rising magnificently above it. A letter from the court in Dresden to the local steward Crusius from 1753 contains the exhortation to assist Bellotto and to ensure that he encounters no obstacles while recording Pirna and its environs. The artist's eleven views of Pirna, taken from greatly differing angles (but always showing Sonnenstein Castle), number among his most beautiful works.

The foreground of this *veduta* shows the small harbour at Pirna, which opens onto the Elbe. The pool was only used to store river-barges in winter; ships loaded with goods would moor downriver, beyond the customs house, on the corner to the far right, which stands to this day. The *veduta* shows few of the town's better-known buildings: the castle rises sublimely above it, and the small guardhouses can clearly be seen on the tips of the bastions. Partly obscured by trees, the Marienkirche is just visible at the end of a row of houses.

The main fascination of this view, however, lies in the row of small, simple buildings set parallel to the picture plane, some half-timbered, some in plain masonry, but all shown fairly close up with their sheds and outhouses, washing and stacked wood. Bellotto performs a daring artistic feat by casting these shabby buildings, so central to the composition, totally in shadow. The contrast with the views of the stately buildings of Dresden (and later those of Vienna and Munich) could scarcely be greater: here the pictorial quality does not lie in the refined beauty of the scene represented, but in its nooks and crannies and general dilapidation. Netherlandish painting of the seventeenth century frequently used such effects, as in the *contre-jour* paintings of Albert Cuyp, the depictions of simple farmer's huts in Rembrandt's graphic works, or the paintings of Cornelis Decker. It is precisely the mention of these representations in the art theories of an academician like Gerard de Lairesse that sparked the debate about whether refined subjects or the results of decay should be termed 'picturesque'.[1] Bellotto does not dwell on this, but simply paints a less obviously attractive side of Pirna, and in so doing elevates it to the status of great art. During the same period Bellotto reproduced a painting by Jan van der Heyden from the collection of the Prime Minister, Count Heinrich Brühl, in Dresden, as a large etching; this work shows a noticeable similarity to this view of Pirna in its subject and structure. Indeed, Bellotto underlines here the 'Netherlandish' character of his Pirna *vedute* by adding elements typical of genre painting: laundry is being hung out to dry in the foreground, using a gnarled willow behind a hut as a clothes-pole. Further to the right, a boat is landing, and the boatman is in the process of casting a rope to some men ashore. To the far left, however, where the *veduta* brings the castle, church and wooden shacks tightly together, a herdsman has driven his cattle to drink in the shallow waters. Bellotto takes this group from a pastoral scene by the Netherlandish artist Nicolaes Berchem, an image published in Venice with the poetic caption: 'Senza pensier sol della Mandra ho cura'.[2] GJMW

33
Count Pietro Rotari (Verona 1707 – St Petersburg 1762)
King Augustus III of Poland, 1755

Oil on canvas,
108 × 86 cm

Collection Prince Johann
Georg (died 1938), Inv. no.
S II/1, no. 111; Schloss
Wachwitz, no. 1094; to the
Gemäldegalerie after 1945,
Inv. no. S 451; bought 1999

Inv. no. 99/77 (pendant
to Inv. no. 99/78); replica
shortly after 1755

LITERATURE
Sponsel 1906, pp.65ff.,
nos 141, 142. Madrid 1998,
no. 29. Venice 1998, pp.97,
223, no. 143. Columbus
1999, no. 29. Weber 1999A,
pp.30ff., 75, no. II, 1 B. Dijon
2001, no. 22. Hamburg 2002,
no. 5.

Frederick Augustus was born in 1696, the son of Frederick Augustus I, Elector of Saxony, who from 1697 was King Augustus II (the Strong) of Poland. During his educational travels from 1711 to 1719 through Germany, Switzerland, Italy and France, the Prince Elector converted to Catholicism in 1712 while at Bologna. In 1719 he married the Austrian Archduchess Maria Josepha and in 1733 succeeded his father to the throne as Elector of Saxony and King of Poland. His reign saw a blossoming of the arts in Dresden, not only the visual arts, but also music, opera and architecture. The large number of paintings that Augustus III acquired brought the Königlichen Gemäldegalerie to a position of international renown, not least with the purchase of Raphael's *Sistine Madonna* from Piacenza (1754). The outbreak of the Seven Years War in 1756 brought these activities to a halt. Augustus III died in Dresden on 5 October 1763.

Rotari's portrait shows the monarch wearing his breastplate under a blue coat and supporting his left hand on his staff, with before him part of his ermine robe. Set resplendently on his chest is the Catholic Order of the Golden Fleece, and almost completely obscured on the lower left is the Polish Order of the White Eagle hanging on a blue ribbon.

Rotari evidently drew on several previous works for this painting: a late three-quarter-length portrait of the King that is known only from an engraving by Georges-Frédéric Schmidt, based on Louis de Silvestre, dated 1743; and two full-length versions in Dresden and Versailles. In the position of the head, seen from slightly below, Rotari is largely following the model of Anton Raphael Mengs, who portrayed the King in pastels in 1744. The differences in the two works reveal how the King aged in the intervening ten years. Compared to the large portraits that Louis de Silvestre painted of such rulers, still fully in the tradition of the *portrait d'apparat* of a Hyacinthe Rigaud, Rotari presents the King in a smaller format and a tighter view, thereby bringing him closer to the viewer. Whereas previously the insignia of power – crowns, sceptres and decorations – might have been ostentatiously displayed, Rotari's approach to portraiture is here quite plain and simple; the ermine robe has been laid aside, the Order of the White Eagle is scarcely visible, and the painter dispenses totally with columns and heavy drapes. The diminution of the attributes and the formal aspects of the picture in order to concentrate on the person's physiognomy shows that Rotari was part of an astonishingly early development that was to lead to the 'enlightened' portrait after the Seven Years War.

In 1768 Giuseppe Canale made an engraving of Rotari's portrait, on which he noted: 'Peint en 1755 par le Comte Pierre Rotari'. The original was at once reproduced a number of times. An unknown copyist, whose excellent work was done with a gentle brush that at times produced a porcelain-like smoothness and differed considerably from Rotari's techniques, was responsible for the present portrait. It has so far not been possible to ascertain the whereabouts of the original of the portrait of Augustus III. GJMW

34

Count Pietro Rotari (Verona 1707 – St Petersburg 1762)

Queen Maria Josepha, Wife of King Augustus III of Poland, 1755

Oil on canvas, 108 × 86 cm

Collection Prinz Johann
Georg (died 1938), Inv. no.
S II/1, no. 112; Schloss
Wachwitz, no. 1086; to the
Gemäldegalerie after 1945,
Inv. no. S 453, bought 1999

Inv. no. 99/78 (pendant
to Inv. no. 99/77); replica
shortly after 1755

LITERATURE
Sponsel 1906, p.67, no. 144.
Madrid 1998, no. 30.
Columbus 1999, no. 30.
Weber 1999A, pp.78ff., no. II,
2 B. Dijon 2001, no. 23.
Hamburg 2002, no. 6.

Maria Josepha, Archduchess of Austria, was born in 1699 in Vienna as the daughter of the subsequent Kaiser Joseph I. In 1719 she married the Saxon Prince Elector Frederick Augustus in Dresden, an occasion for which Frederick Augustus's father Augustus the Strong staged a series of court festivities of enormous splendour. The marriage was blessed with fifteen children, of whom several died at a tender age. Maria Josepha propagated Catholicism in Protestant Saxony, more specifically the form espoused by the Jesuits (almost all of her children were given either Ignatius or Francis Xavier as their patron saint). She died in 1757 in Dresden, a year after the commencement of the Seven Years War.

This portrait shows the Queen at the age of 56. She wears the cross and ribbon of the Russian Order of St Catherine, as well as the Austrian Order of the Starry Cross. Among her exquisite items of jewellery she wears a drop-shaped brilliant in her hair that is held in place by a clip shaped like a black eagle. This famous gem is still preserved in the Green Vault in Dresden to this day. The miniature portrait on her richly adorned bracelet shows her husband, King Augustus III.

The painting conforms to the concept of the eloquent portrait; the sitter directs her gaze at the viewer, and her hand points to the portrait of her husband, the picture's pendant. Rotari again borrowed from Mengs, from his pastel of the Queen dating from 1744. Rotari's cool, classicist approach is indebted to the style of Pompeo Batoni, with whose work he had become familiar in Rome. The painting was executed by the same copyist as its counterpart. GJMW

35

Giovanni Battista Tiepolo (Venice 1696 – Madrid 1770)

The Vision of St Anne, 1759

Oil on canvas, 244 × 120 cm

Inscribed lower right on the pier of the bridge: GIO.BTTA. / TIEPOLO.O. / 1759

Etched by Lorenzo Tiepolo

Acquired 1926

Gal. no. 580 A

LITERATURE
Levey 1988, p. 221. Gemin and Pedrocco 1993, p. 469. Udine 1996, p. 170, no. 22. Weber 1998B, pp. 12ff.

NOTES
1 The large *Banquet of Cleopatra* is now in Melbourne, Australia; the *Caesar Contemplating the Head of Pompey* is now missing. Weber 1996, pp. 183ff.
2 *Maecenas Presenting the Arts to Augustus* is now in St Petersburg and *The Triumph of Flora* in San Francisco.
3 Inscribed verso: 'Modello originale di Tiepolo per la tavola dell'altare nel convento di Santa Chiara in Cividale. Comprato dalla galleria Barlese Tiepolo per lire sessantatre il 23 maggio 1808.'
4 Udine 1996, p. 170.

Giovanni Battista Tiepolo was foremost among the artists who enjoyed the special patronage of Count Francesco Algarotti. While purchasing and commissioning works for Augustus III in Venice, Algarotti managed first of all to secure Tiepolo's large *Banquet of Cleopatra* for Dresden. Of the subsequent six paintings in the same format ordered from among others Piazzetta, Amigoni and Pittoni, another was by Tiepolo. Augustus III had both Tiepolos brought in 1755 to the gallery in Schloss Hubertusburg, where they fell into Prussian hands at the end of the Seven Years War and were finally auctioned off in 1765 in Amsterdam.[1] Two smaller paintings by Tiepolo, presents from Algarotti to the Prime Minister, Count Heinrich Brühl, also failed to remain in Dresden.[2] It is understandable why after such losses Hans Posse took pains in the 1920s to acquire more works by Tiepolo: in 1926 *The Vision of St Anne*, and in 1927 the large work *The Triumph of Amphitrite* (Gal. no. 580 B).

The Vision of St Anne was painted in 1759 for the church of Santa Chiara at the Benedictine monastery in Cividale, Friuli. The building can be made out in the small image in the background, together with the Santuario di Castelmonte and the old bridge over the River Natisone. The painting was removed from the church in 1810 and finally came onto the Milan art market in 1845, from whence it entered the collections of Don Agostino Quarzoli and, from 1890 to 1900, of Benigno Crespi, until it was auctioned in 1914 by Georges Petit in Paris. The Crespi Collection also contained an oil sketch by Tiepolo of the painting, which is now in the keeping of the Rijksmuseum in Amsterdam.[3]

In this strongly vertical composition, Tiepolo develops three distinct levels, one above the other: kneeling at the front is St Anne, who holds out her arms while gazing up to heaven; her husband, Joachim, who is shown behind a balustrade with his hands folded in prayer, looks in the same direction. Borne aloft on a cloud by angels, the young Mary is suspended above them. She too looks up to heaven and God the Father, who appears there leaning on the globe with his arms outstretched. According to legend, Anne was already advanced in years when she unexpectedly became pregnant with Mary, whose special status as the future mother of the Son of God is highlighted by her mystical elevation and the presence of God the Father. The Bible does not tell us of the events that Tiepolo so effectively stages in his *Vision of St Anne*. As early as 1839, Fabio di Maniago praised the work as a 'bizzarra invenzione', and simultaneously extolled its 'magico colorito'.[4]

Tiepolo shows us here the full glory of his light palette, most especially in the area centring on the Virgin, which is charged with light. His rational working methods – no doubt first tested in frescoes – speak from his technique of applying areas of colour approximately and then heightening them with his draughtsman's eye using black lines. Tiepolo's virtuoso methods make this visionary work utterly convincing. GJMW

The
French
School

36

Nicolas Poussin (Les Andelys 1594 – Rome 1665)
Pan and Syrinx, 1637

Oil on canvas,
106.5 × 82 cm

1742 via de Brais, Secretary
to the Saxon Legation, from
the collection of the art-
dealer Dubreuil in Paris;
cursorily entered on p.318
of Steinhäuser's eighth
inventory of paintings in 8°
(octavo) as 'before 1741',
with 44 other paintings that
arrived in 1742 from Paris,
nos 3210–53; inventory 1754,
no. 707 (French and German
School 'On the columns')

Gal. no. 718

LITERATURE
Félibien 1685–88, vol. 2,
p. 328. Riedel and Wenzel
1765, G. E. no. 624.
Argenville 1768, vol. 4,
p. 49. Lehninger 1782, p.221.
Hübner 1856, no. 622.
Woermann 1887, no. 718.
Friedländer 1914, pp.31, 56.
Grautoff 1914, vol. 1, pp.
134ff.; vol. 2, no. 66. Magne
1914, no. 90. Posse 1929,
pp. 355ff. Friedländer 1965,
vol. 1, pp.136ff. Blunt
1966/67, vol. 2, p.150, no. 171.
Knab 1967–68, p.21. Badt
1969, pp. 164, 304ff., 518ff.
Dresden 1972, no. 79.
Thuillier 1974, no. 104.
Wild 1980, no. 75. Wright
1984, no. 97. Marx 1994A,
pp. 163ff. Dijon 2001, no. 74.
Hamburg 2002, no. 36.

NOTES
1 'Je me suis plu à peindre
le sujet de la fable de Pan
et de Syrinx que j'envoie
à M. de La Fleur mon
confrère. Si j'ai jamais fait
quelque chose de bien,
je crois que c'est dans la
manière dont ce sujet est
traité. Je l'ai peint avec
amour et tendresse. Le
sujet le voulait ainsi.'
2 '...faire voir à Paris, au
même moment, trois
tableaux profondément
différents par le style et
le coloris'.
3 'Le Poussin avait de
grands égard à traiter
différemment tous les sujets
qu'il représentait, non

With regard to this painting, Jacques Thuillier cites a fragment of a letter written in 1637 by Nicolas Poussin to Jacques Stella. The letter gives us the date of the work, the fact that it was received by the painter Nicolas Guillaume de La Fleur, and that Poussin painted it with 'love and tenderness' because he considered that the subject merited it.[1]

Poussin mentions other paintings in this letter to Stella, each of which was painted in a different manner. His aim was to show three paintings in Paris at the same moment, each profoundly different in style and coloration.[2] André Félibien has already remarked on Poussin's works from 1637 that 'Poussin went to great lengths to vary his treatment for every subject he undertook, not only by use of different expressions, but also by painting some more delicately and others more strongly'.[3]

In the same context, Anthony Blunt notes that our knowledge of Poussin's work 'in the last years of the 1630s is much more abundant than for the preceding period, but it is not easy to interpret. For the year 1637, for instance, Félibien assigns five paintings, of which one, the *Hercules and Deianira*, is only known from drawings; but all the others – *Pan and Syrinx*, *Armida Carrying Off Rinaldo*, the Louvre *Camillus* and the Ellesmere-Sutherland *Moses* – are executed in different manners. The *Pan and Syrinx* at Dresden is probably the earliest.'

The subject of our picture comes from Ovid's *Metamorphoses* (I, 688–712). Pan, the goat-limbed shepherd-god, lusted after Syrinx and went in pursuit of her. The beautiful nymph, unable to return his love, fled to her father, the river-god Ladon. She asked her sisters, one of whom appears at the far left of the painting, to transform her into a reed at the moment Pan reached her. Resigned, Pan took the reed and fashioned it into a flute with pipes of different lengths, which is referred to either as pan-pipes, after him, or as a 'syrinx', after her.

Poussin chooses the moment in which Pan has almost caught the fleeing nymph: but movement becomes pose, time stands still, and Syrinx escapes through her transformation. Despite the terpsichorean harmony of the two, their contrary desires are convincingly written into their figures: the joyous yearning and onwards urge of Pan, and Syrinx's timid wish to preserve herself. The sensual vitality of the shepherd-god and the chaste beauty of the nymph are also clearly characterised by the artist's choice of colours: Pan, a reddish brown, and Syrinx pale in colour.

Flying above the pair is Cupid as a winged boy holding a torch and a lead-tipped arrow, which he is about to cast at Syrinx. Ovid tells us that Cupid had various arrow-tips: a golden tip awakened love, while that of lead had the opposite effect. In Dresden, Jean August Lehninger wrote in 1782: 'Poussin was an excellent draughtsman, a great historian and poet, who was wise in his compositions, never positioning a figure until he was sure of its purpose; a great landscape painter; no-one has better succeeded in expressing the various effects of nature.'[4]

The dramatic events of the pursuit and the transformation take place within a landscape suffused with light; a light which, with its delicate, atmospheric *sfumato*, would have been more fitting for an idyll than this dramatic scene. The putti at the bottom of the picture cast themselves aside in fright. The tree trunk on the

seulement par les
différentes expressions,
mais encore par les
diverses manières de
peindre les unes plus
délicates, les autres plus
fortes.'

4 'Poussin étoit excellent
dessinateur, grand
historien, grand poët,
sage compositeur, ne
mettant une seule figure
qu'il n'en connut la
nécessité; grand
paysagiste; personne n'a
mieux exprimé les divers
effets de la nature.'

far right has been painted over Pan's hoof. Evidently Poussin added the tree
at a later stage, to produce greater articulation in the picture's spatial structure.

The river-god Ladon checks the two central protagonists, allowing the picture's
suspense and dynamism to culminate at its centre. His face, reminiscent of that of
the Antique sculpture of Laocoön in his death throes, seems to bear the ineluctable
suffering of Antique tragedies, with a depth and emotion that goes beyond all
human contingency. From the moment of its discovery in 1506 in Rome, the
Hellenistic sculpture of the Trojan priest and his sons entwined by serpents awoke
the especial interest of artists, for it showed a restrained formulation of agonising
death that was valid for all time. HM

37

Claude Lorrain, originally known as Claude Gellée (Chamagne 1600 – Rome 1682)

Landscape with the Flight into Egypt, 1647

Inscribed lower left: CLAVDE IV[EF] ROMA 16[47] (IVEF = invenit et fecit: devised and painted by Claude)

Oil on canvas, 102 × 134 cm

Described in the *Liber Veritatis* (LV 110) as painted for 'Mr Parasson of Lyons' (according to Michel, one of the Perrachon brothers, financiers who had connections with Mazarin); Cardinal Mazarin (not described in the inventory of 1653 [?]; inventory of 1661, no. 1289: 'A landscape by Claude Lorrain showing a riverscape with shepherds playing the flute by a well, three feet three inches tall, four feet wide'); Comtesse de Verrue; from her to Comte de Nocé, together with *Landscape with Acis and Galatea* by Gellée (Dresden) in exchange for Rubens's *The Conversion* (copy, Dresden); from Nocé on 12 April 1725 to Graf Karl Heinrich von Hoym, together with *Landscape with Acis and Galatea*, entered in the 1726 inventory in the principal room of the first floor at his town palace in Rue Cassette, Paris, as no. 297, with provenance: Mazarin, Verrue, Nocé; 1731 still in Paris, mentioned 1736 by von Hoym in a list for an auction at place unnamed to be held on his death; to the Dresden Gemäldegalerie between the revision of the Guarienti inventory 1747–50, wherein not mentioned, and that of 1754, where catalogued for the first time as Gal. no. 730

LITERATURE
Pichon 1880, vol. 1, p.186; vol. 2, pp.60ff., 72, nos 297, 325. Menz 1962, p.262, fig. 2.263. Roethlisberger 1968, p.248. Kitson 1978, p.119. Roethlisberger 1979, vol. 1, pp. 273ff., LV 110, 9ll, fig. 191. Roethlisberger 1986, p.109, no. 175, fig. p.108. Marx, in Dresden 1992, p.253, plate 29. Michel 1999, pp.130ff., 149ff. (nos 279, 280, 283), 251, 256 (nos 122–23), 333, 343 (no. 178), 594ff. (no. 1289). Dijon 2001, no. 71. Hamburg 2002, no. 37.

Graf Hoym, the chargé d'affaires and later ambassador of Saxony-Poland to France from 1720 to 1728, had no less than ten paintings by Claude Lorrain in his town palace in Rue Cassette in Paris. The first, of which Roethlisberger was able to detect a number of overt copies, came from Cardinal Mazarin's astonishing collection; he had received it from a certain 'Parasson' in Lyons, whose name appears in the *Liber Veritatis* next to the drawing of the picture. It is possible that the painting was originally conceived with *Landscape with Shepherds*, now in the keeping of the Metropolitan Museum of Art in New York. In that case, the pair of pictures must have been separated at a very early date, because only the one in Dresden was named in the Mazarin inventory of 1661, in connection with another painting.

The Flight into Egypt appears in the background to the left, framed by a group of trees. Claude was fond of this subject, yet he rarely approached it in such a discreet manner. The holy family, watched over by an angel, seem to be there almost by chance amid this classically inspired jewel-box of a landscape. The overall effect recalls a pastoral scene from Virgil, which brings us to the three figures in Antique attire in the foreground: a shepherd playing a pipe, a seated washerwoman, and to the right a woman collecting water from a spring.

A herd of cattle and goats, including a kid falling from a rock, approaches them to quench their thirst in the river. Everything unites to convey a vision of a harmonious world with a lively river, the font of life, flowing through its heart. Although the work is lent precision by the detailing of the different species of tree, it is the light that consolidates the whole: the clarity of the breaking day unfolding from the left – as always Claude has painted the early morning – brings the forms out of the shade and submerges the distance in a milky haze.

Graf Hoym, who paid a high price for the picture, praised it as a work from 'Claude's best period'. Painted in 1647 in Rome, where the artist had made his home over twenty years beforehand, the Dresden landscape proves his maturity and shows how he was able to synthesise the sensitivity to nature evinced in northern painting with the classical idealism of a Carracci or Poussin. From 1640 onwards, the artist enjoyed a growing renown that spread from Italy to France and England. Hoym's collection characterises Claude's posthumous evaluation in almost allegorical form. Of the ten paintings by Claude that he collected in Paris during the 1720s, five had found their way across the Channel within a century, including the two magnificent pictures that came into the possession of the Duke of Sutherland, *Landscape with Moses and the Burning Bush* and the *Landscape with Ezekiel Weeping in the Ruins of Tyre*.

East of the Rhine, Claude's paintings are relatively scarce. Three landscapes were commissioned by Franz Mayer, adviser to the Elector of Bavaria, in Regensburg (two are now in Munich, the third in Dulwich Picture Gallery). During the eighteenth century, the Count Palatine of Zweibrücken owned two (both are now in Munich), and Landgrave Wilhelm VIII of Hessen-Kassel had four (these were later to arrive in St Petersburg). German museums that have made more recent purchases include Berlin, Cologne, Frankfurt, Hamburg and Karlsruhe. MCS

38

Antoine Watteau (Valenciennes 1684 – Nogent-sur-Marne 1721)

The Festival of Love, 1717 (?)

Oil on canvas,
61 × 75 cm

First in the Guarienti
inventory 1747–50, no. 1747;
in the printed gallery
catalogues since 1765,
G. E. 488

Gal. no. 782

LITERATURE
Schäfer 1860, vol. 2, pp. 316ff.
Rosenberg 1896, p. 86.
Zimmermann 1912, p. 189.
Hildebrandt 1922, pp. 25, 106,
121, 149. Pilon 1924, p. 157.
Adhémar 1950, no. 194.
Kurth 1956. Aragon and
Cocteau 1957, pp. 155, 195.
Nemilowa 1964, p. 138.
Knapp 1968, pp. 249ff. Ferré
1972, no. A 28. Michel 1984,
p. 231. Dresden 1992, p. 410.
Columbus 1999, no. 97.
Munich 2000, pp. 196ff.

NOTES
1 Boerlin-Brodbeck 1973,
  p. 222.
2 See Paris 1977, p. 180
  (Chantal), p. 120 (Dorival).
3 Phillips 1895, p. 85.
4 Rosenberg 1806, p. 107,
  figs 15, 16.

Set in a curiously weightless landscape, an irregular row of trees enters the picture at an angle, affording us glimpses of meadows, stretches of water and buildings, with beyond a distant hill and a plane that vanishes into the depths. We see a number of couples, some reclining, some out walking, and a child and a small dog, both at the centre of the picture if not immediately visible. Opposite the soft, hazy trees that dominate the left half of the picture, the right-hand side is commanded by a statue of Venus, who has confiscated a quiver full of arrows from her son, Cupid.

A happy moment has been caught here by the painter's art, like a snapshot that captures a fleeting moment from the past – a gaze over a shoulder, a spontaneous gesture – and lends it permanence. Yet it would be absurd to assume that this scene was based on a real occurrence: the picture is a poetic invention by a painter, is itself the experience, and not a depiction.

A *Bacchanal* by Rubens has been identified as the model for a number of similar compositions, a painting that for its part goes back to Titian. Watteau's picture has, by turn, had its own influence, and it is easy to understand why it attracted the admiration of a painter like Auguste Renoir. Yvonne Boerlin-Brodbeck has noted in this context that the *Festival of Love*, with its 'row of bright, lightly plumed trees', is like a foretaste of 'those landscapes of the nineteenth century in which a vanishing line likewise enters the picture at an angle and lends depth to the content, woven as it is in coloured light'.[1] Suzanne Chantal has demonstrated an even more immediate 'echo' of the Dresden painting in Renoir's *Moulin de la Galette* (Musée d'Orsay, Paris), and we must thank Bernard Dorival for pointing out that Edouard Manet was spellbound by the painting as early as 1856, during his visit to Dresden.[2]

Just how little importance Watteau attached to faithful representations of reality can be seen in the reversal, or at least inclination, of the perspectives. The spatial relationship of the figures remains unclear, and the couple looking over their shoulders at the centre seem to have no spatial connection to the people in the foreground. The large, floating pair of figures bears no relation to the trees, which gradually diminish into the picture's depths. The space in this painting has not been constructed by means of perspective, nor by changes in hue from brown to green to blue; it is simply a presentiment that vanishes amidst delicate gradations of colour.

At the same time, the composition is compellingly simple: the lower border of the trees' foliage and the alignment of the heads, from those of the gentlemen wearing berets to that of Venus, create the diagonal lines that dominate the picture, although their point of intersection remains empty. The painting in Dresden differs in this from Watteau's corresponding drawing at the Art Institute of Chicago. In that work, the groups of figures are arranged differently: the couples on the two sides are positioned further apart, so that the couple on the right stand before the plinth of the statue of Venus, and the couple on the left are more clearly removed from the centre of the picture; on closer inspection, the groups themselves differ fundamentally.

Compared to both the central group looking back over their shoulders, and to the horizon, the Venus in the drawing rises much higher, making the figures appear smaller and the space more real. The area to the right, above the sculpture, shows open sky in the Dresden painting, and the overall motion of the picture seems to flow in that direction. The drawing, on the other hand, has tall trees on its right edge, and the couple at the centre has come to a proper standstill: the scene has an inner harmony and tranquillity while the Dresden painting is full of turbulence. A look at the area between the base of the sculpture and the figures says everything: what is space, and what is surface?

It has long been known that the Venus in the Dresden picture is also to be found in the *Embarkation for Cythera* (Schloss Charlottenburg, Berlin). The statue of Venus in the Chicago drawing is similar, but again different to that of the two paintings. The sculpture in the Berlin picture is integrated into the overall composition and seems smaller as a whole; it appears curiously isolated and out of proportion in the Dresden painting. The presence of the sculpture in the two paintings was important for the dating of the Dresden work; because the Berlin painting has been dated at around 1718/19, it has been assumed that the *Festival of Love* was painted at about the same time. Its general stylistic features support such a dating.

Montagni, for example, dated the *Festival of Love* to 1717, earlier than the Berlin painting. Claude Phillips attributed it more generally to Watteau's late period, adding significantly that his pupil, Jean-Baptiste Pater, was indebted to precisely these late works, with their delicate use of colour.[3] Adolf Rosenberg assumed the date to be 1718–20; it was beyond question for him that the statue of Venus in the Dresden painting was a repetition of the figure from the Berlin *Embarkation for Cythera*.[4]

It is neither possible here to give a definitive answer on the exact relationship between the Chicago drawing and the paintings in Berlin and Dresden, nor to say whether the small picture *The Faux Pas* at the Louvre in Paris, which depicts a small group from the *Festival of Love* as a single motif, served as a study for the painting or was painted at a later date. Yet ultimately the fascinating beauty of this picture, with its mysterious lightness and poetic delicacy, remains untouched by such detailed questions. The art of Antoine Watteau is difficult to explain in historical terms, even if the period of the Régence, to which the painting in Dresden assuredly belongs, was characterised by a rebellion against the stiffness and grandeur that had typified the latter years of the Sun King's reign prior to his death in 1715. HM

39

Antoine Pesne (Paris 1683 – Berlin 1757)

Girl with Pigeons, 1728

Signed lower left:
Pesne fecit 1728

Oil on canvas,
76 × 61 cm

Delivered in 1728 by Pesne;
first appearance in the
Dresden inventory of
paintings 1722–28, A 1975

Gal. no. 773

LITERATURE
Riedel and Wenzel 1765,
G. E. no. 65. Lehninger 1782,
p. 325. Schäfer 1860, vol. 2,
p. 313, no. 662. Parthey
1861–64, vol. 2, p. 245, no.
140. Colombier 1930, no. 40.
Holzhausen 1940, p. 65.
Eckardt 1957, no. 18.
Berckenhagen 1958, no.
477a. Potsdam 1983, no. 32.
Börsch-Supan 1986, p. 17.
Columbus 1999, no. 65.
Hamburg 2002, no. 38.

NOTES
1 '[Portrait] de sa fille, ayant
  un Chapeau de paille sur
  la tête & tenant deux
  Colombes; demi figure.'
2 Honthorst's painting
  was on view at the 1993
  Banco Bilbao Viszcaya
  exhibition, 'La Pintura
  Holandesa del Siglo de
  Oro: La escuela de
  Utrecht'.
3 Sotheby's London,
  20 April 1994, lot no. 88.

'[Portrait] of the artist's daughter, with a straw hat on her head and holding two doves; half-length.'[1] Pesne's painting was described thus in the *Catalogue* issued by the Gemäldegalerie in 1765, and in the *Abrégé de la vie des peintres dont les tableaux composent la Galerie Electorale de Dresde…* of 1782.

Wilhelm Schäfer saw the painting differently in 1860: 'This attractive, nicely conceived and flatteringly lit painting with its delightful colours shows us a young French (?) countrywoman (probably from the vicinity of Paris), who under the protection of her straw hat is proffering her goods as a *Marchande paysanne*. For apart from the pair of pigeons she is clutching in her hands, she also has two young hens sitting there in the straw. The clair-obscure of her lively face shaded by the straw hat is quite exquisite.'

However accurate Schäfer's observations are, his realistic description is erroneous: we are not looking at a scene spotted by chance in the vicinity of Paris, but at a composition made in the studio. Thus it is not unlikely that the old catalogues are correct when they state that the picture depicts the artist's young daughter, albeit in the guise of a young rural woman.

A deeper interpretation suggested by Helmut Börsch-Supan, which focuses on the pigeons – an attribute of Venus – to turn 'the country girl into a goddess of love', seems unconvincing when one remembers that they are accompanied by a couple of hens, as Schäfer had noted in 1860. But we can agree wholeheartedly with another of Börsch-Supan's observations: 'The fresh, natural air of this creature, together with the painter's individual touch, sets this work apart from those pictures so often encountered during this period of aristocratic ladies dressed as shepherdesses.'

The face cast into semi-shadow by the hat brim recalls Rembrandt's portrait of Saskia as a young woman in the Dresden Gemäldegalerie (Gal. no. 1556), although distinct differences exist. The picture's connections with Dutch seventeenth-century painting have been overlooked until now: the parallels alone to Gerard van Honthorst's picture in the Centraal Museum in Utrecht are astonishing, and cannot be the result of pure chance; Pesne must have been familiar with such compositions, perhaps through engraved reproductions.[2]

A few *pentimenti* above the pigeons are visible to the naked eye and indicate that the artist altered his concept while painting the work. A copy attributed to Domenico Fedeli, known as Maggiotto (1713–1794), was sold in 1994.[3] HM

40

Louis de Silvestre (Paris or Sceaux 1675 – Paris 1760)

Christ on the Cross Formed by Clouds, 1734

Oil on canvas, 73 × 52 cm

Purchased in 1994 at the Dorotheum auction house in Vienna

Gal. no. 94/02

LITERATURE
Marx 1994B. Salmon 1997, no. 11. Marx, in Dresden 2001B, no. 11.

NOTE
1 'Ce que l'on voit dans ce tableau, représentant un Christ en Croix formé par des nuées au milieu d'un ciel bleu, a esté vu au ciel du coté du soleil couchant à la vigne de Rotschberg à six heures et un quart du soir le 19 May 1734. Sa durée parfaite a esté d'un quart d'heure. Les spectateurs étaient: / Mr. l'abbé Pirenne.C. [Catholique] / Mr. Bildstein le fils et son valet. L. [Luthérien.] / Mr. Favrier. C. / Md. Embry. C. / Md. Richter veuve. L / Les vignerons, les vigneronnes et le jardinier. L. / Md. Sylvestre et ses deux filles. C. / et moi Louis Sylvestre qui l'ayt peint tel que l'on voit ici. Les personnes cy-dessus nommées dont la plupart l'ont vu peindre sont convenues de la parfaite ressemblance autant que l'art peut representer une chose aussi admirable et extraordinaire.'

This work, purchased in 1994, is a previously unknown sketch for a monumental work by Silvestre measuring 291 × 201 cm. The full-scale version is described at length in an inscription, which can equally well be applied to the present sketch: 'What one sees in this picture, a representation of Christ on the cross formed from clouds against a blue sky, was witnessed in the heavens next to the setting sun in the vineyards at Rotschberg at a quarter past six in the evening on 19 May 1734. The cross was perfectly formed for a quarter of an hour. Those present were: / M. l'Abbé Pirenne. C. [Catholic] / The younger M. Bildstein and his valet. L. [Lutheran] / M. Favrier. C. / Mme Embry. C. / The widow Richter. L / The vine-tenders and the gardener. L. / Mme Sylvestre and her two daughers. C. / and myself, Louis Sylvestre, who painted what can be seen here. The persons here mentioned, of whom the majority saw me paint the work, confirm that this is as true a resemblance as art can render of something so admirable and extraordinary.'[1]

The picture differs fundamentally from all of Louis de Silvestre's other works. It strikes the viewer as disturbingly modern, and seems to be a mystery both in compositional terms and as regards the intensity of the colours. Only with an explanation of why the painting was done, as is related in the inscription on the large painting, and the knowledge that the artist was inspired to paint the picture by the actual sight of such a cloud formation, can the viewer understand why the work seems to flaunt all artistic convention.

A small pastel copy of the painting made by the Saxon Princess Maria Amalia (1724–1760) is in the keeping of the Bayerische Nationalmuseum in Munich. In 1738 Maria Amalia married the Spanish Viceroy, who resided in Naples and was later to become King Carlos III of Spain. She made the pastel copy in Dresden a year before her marriage, apparently as a copy of the sketch, although the inscription on the rear names the large canvas as her model. The small differences that exist between the sketch and the finished painting – in the clouds, in the crucifix and in the superscription – can also be seen between Maria Amalia's pastel and the large painting. We can assume that the small sketch must have been well-known at that time at the court in Dresden.

Was everything that Silvestre shows here really to be seen in the sky, or was he perhaps influenced by older visual traditions? There were, after all, important precedents in European painting for depicting Christ on the cross as a solitary, monumental figure towering into the sky and giving the scene a cosmic dimension. The effect of the light, the use of colour, and the cloud-formation of the image remain, however, the result of a natural phenomenon: the clouds break open and the view into the measureless blue of the sky beyond suddenly becomes the backdrop to the slender, finely modelled and plastic form of Christ crucified. HM

41

Pierre Subleyras (Saint-Gilles, Languedoc 1699 – Rome 1749)

Christ at the House of Simon the Pharisee, *c.* 1737

Oil on canvas,
50.5 × 122 cm

1739, as a gift from the artist
to the Saxon Prince Elector
Frederick Christian; in the
catalogues of the Dresden
Gemäldegalerie since 1765,
G. E. 315

Gal. no. 789

LITERATURE
Lehninger 1782, p. 238.
Fiorillo 1805, vol. 3, p. 331.
Voss 1924, p. 643.
Winckelmann 1925, vol. 1,
p. 270. Paris 1987, no. 35.
Dresden 1992, p. 367. Madrid
1998, no. 69. Columbus 1999,
no. 76. Dijon 2001, no. 75.

NOTES
1 Sächsisches
  Hauptstaatsarchiv
  Dresden, Ihrer Hoheit
  des Königl. Chur-
  Printzens Herrn
  Friedrichs Aufenthalt
  zu Rom betr. A° 1739,
  vol. 3, loc. 768, p. 185.
2 Femmel 1980, no. K 72.

This picture is based on the story in the Gospel of St Luke (VII, 36–50) in which Christ was invited to dine with Simon the Pharisee. 'And behold, a woman in the city, which was a sinner, when she knew that Jesus sat at meat in the Pharisee's house, brought an alabaster box of ointment. And stood at his feet behind him weeping, and began to wash his feet with tears, and did wipe them with the hairs of her head…And he said to the woman, "Thy faith hath saved thee…"' The painting is directly linked with a large composition at the Louvre in Paris, which Subleyras painted in Rome from about 1735 to 1737 for the refectory of Santa Maria Nuova, a monastery in Asti, Piedmont. This work was chiefly responsible for his fame during the eighteenth century. He made many studies prior to embarking on the picture. Even while working on it he made a number of small versions, including this painting, which should be regarded as a work in its own right. Subleyras attached great importance to the Dresden version; indeed, by presenting it to Frederick Christian of Saxony, the heir to the Elector, he pinned to the work his hopes of a position in Dresden.

In 1739 Frederick Christian sojourned in Rome; he had travelled to Italy as companion to his sister Maria Amalia Christina, who had the year before married King Carlos IV of Naples, who became in 1759 King Carlos III of Spain. Frederick Christian had been charged by his father, King Augustus III, to look in Rome for 'some good artists who are sufficiently talented to be taken into the service of the King in Saxony', as we read in a memoir from Count Moritz Brühl, Chamberlain and the brother of the Saxon Prime Minister, who went to Italy as one of the future Elector's companions. Pierre Subleyras caught their attention the most, and Brühl wrote of him in 1739: 'He is just as good in historical painting as in portraiture, has had success in both fields, and his work has earned him a great reputation, particularly a painting that is 25 foot wide, his *Last Supper*, a sketch of which he has presented to his Royal Majesty as a gift.'[1]

The catalogue to the Subleyras exhibition of 1987 describes the work as 'the large Dresden sketch', adding that it distinguishes itself by a 'very skilful execution' and that it was probably used by the artist 'for the realisation of his large painting for Asti'. Subleyras himself made a large engraving of the painting, which is signed and dated: p. Subleyra inven. Pinxit, et sculp. Romae 1738. A copy of this engraving was kept by Goethe in his personal print collection.[2] HM

The
Netherlandish
School

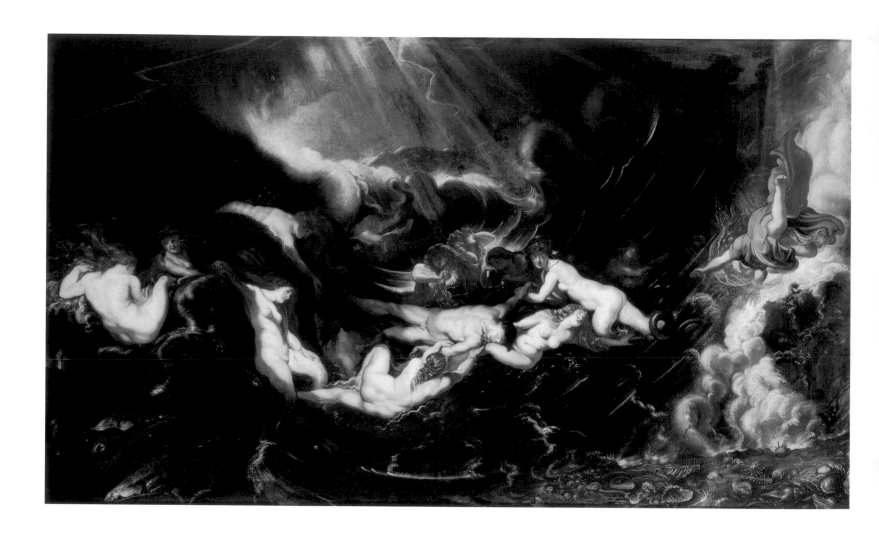

42

Peter Paul Rubens (Siegen 1577 – Antwerp 1640)

Hero and Leander, *c.* 1605

Oil on canvas, 128 × 217 cm

Acquired in 1657 by Wolf Caspar von Klengel in Italy, entered 1659 in the Dresden Kunstkammer inventory by Tobias Beutel; in the 1722–28 inventory, B 1140, as 'Rubens copy, the sea-nymphs with Leander'; until 1832 in the Kunstkammer, then placed in the 'store' of the Gemäldegalerie

Gal. no. 1002

LITERATURE
Jaffé 1977, pp.69ff. Müller Hofstede, in Cologne 1977, pp.147ff., under no. 8. Boston 1993, no. 6. Amsterdam 1999, p.17. Hamburg 2002, no. 22.

This early Rubens is based on a little-known literary source popular in seventeenth-century Netherlandish art that has since faded into obscurity: the Hero and Leander epic by the Greek poet Musaeus, which appeared in 1494 in Venice in a Latin translation. Musaeus describes how Leander sets out for the last time to swim the Hellespont in order to visit his beloved, Hero. As the torch that lights his way is doused by the waves, Leander loses his bearings and drowns in the storm-tossed sea. On discovering the corpse of her lover accompanied by nereids the next day, Hero plunges from her tower into the sea.

In the Dresden version, Rubens gives additional intensity to the story by combining consecutive events to produce one highly dramatic scene: the death of Leander, the way his pale, lifeless body is accompanied by thirteen nereids through the churning waves, and finally Hero's plunge into the depths. The subject of Rubens's composition is, in fact, the human body in extremes of movement. Hero and the nereids swim, float, glide, fly, twist and writhe, seemingly abandoning themselves through their movements to the waters and the storm. The sole exception is Leander, a lifeless corpse set directly at the picture's centre. This contrast between death and lively animation could not have been depicted more theatrically or to greater effect.

The *Hero and Leander* was painted during Rubens's second stay at the court of Mantua, where he worked from the middle of 1604 until the end of 1605 for Duke Vincenzo Gonzaga. It belongs to a group of at least five works that were evidently painted at this time for the free market, without any definite client. The common feature of these works, among them *The Fall of Phaeton* and *Pharaoh's Army Drowned in the Red Sea*, lies in their portrayal of historical scenes with large numbers of figures, which allowed Rubens to depict powerfully moving bodies in extreme perspectives. The works clearly show the influence on the young Fleming of Michelangelo and Caravaggio, and also in the particular case of *Hero and Leander* of Leonardo and Tintoretto.

A number of conjectures have been made in the past about the identity of the Dresden version of *Hero and Leander*. This general confusion stemmed from the fact that in 1685 a second, smaller version of Rubens's painting had arrived in Dresden from Italy, which from then on was referred to by Tobias Beutel, the director of the Kunstkammer who also received the first version, as the 'real original'. The second *Hero and Leander*, which from 1707 was displayed at the Residenz, was listed however in later Dresden catalogues as a copy based on Rubens; since the nineteenth century it has been listed as missing. UN

43

Peter Paul Rubens (Siegen 1577 – Antwerp 1640)

Diana Returning from the Hunt, *c. 1616*

Oil on canvas, 136 × 184 cm

Acquired 1709 by de Witt in
Antwerp; 1722–28
inventory, A 48; 1741
inventory, 48a; Guarienti
inventory 1747–50, 136; 1754
inventory, 359

Gal. no. 962 A

LITERATURE
Evers 1942, pp.196–201,
no. 137, fig. 109. Larsen 1952,
p.158, figs 73–75. Antwerp
1977, p.103, no. 40. Dresden
1992, p.332. Boston 1993,
pp.30ff., fig. 22.

NOTE
1 Bleyl 1981, pp.56ff.

Rubens returned to Antwerp in 1608 from Italy an extremely well-educated and well-read humanist scholar, and a highly talented artist already enjoying success in his early manhood. He brought with him an interest in the heritage of Antique art and literature that developed into a cornerstone of his thinking and artistic production. After setting up home once more in Antwerp, Rubens devoted himself with unfailing interest to Greek and Roman mythology, which he used for the subjects of many works, mostly as private commissions.

The goddess Diana was evidently of great importance to Rubens in around 1615, for she could be combined with another subject that interested him: the hunt. Moreover, this subject was well received by his royal and aristocratic patrons: game hunting was the exclusive preserve of the ruling class. Rubens produced a number of large-format hunting scenes in 1614/15, many with mythological backdrops.

Rather than emphasising extremes of movement, as is typical of many of Rubens's hunting pictures, the Dresden *Diana Returning from the Hunt* focuses instead on characterising the powerful, beautiful and pensive huntress. Diana, simultaneously the goddess of chastity, stands with her companions before a group of satyrs, who belong to a quite different branch of Rubens's work: Bacchanalia. Diana's hunting spear divides the different worlds of the two groups. And no less different than their appearances and natures are the spoils held by the satyrs on the one side, and by Diana and her companions on the other. The fruit presented in richly laden baskets and the intoxicating wine, combined with the lecherous gazes of these half-naked figures, must be seen as an unambiguous sexual overture. Diana, guardian of female chastity, resists. The birds and the dead hare that she and her nymphs have bagged during the hunt reveal them as the conquerors of the pleasurable indulgence embodied by the friends of Bacchus. A contrary interpretation of the picture is also sometimes found, and as early as in the caption to Schelte a Bolswert's contemporary engraving of this painting (Städelsches Kunstinstitut, Frankfurt am Main) we read: 'And may the drowsy women be a pleasing reward for you: fruit and game go together to make a fine repast.'

No doubt Rubens kept returning to the theme of Diana because it allowed him to depict the finely formed, scantily clad female form. He highlighted the differences between the flesh tones, between the satyrs' furs and Diana's filmy fabrics, and between the hands, the satyrs' coarse and heavy and Diana's fine and soft. The groups of fruit and game in the painting, as well as the dogs, are from the brush of Frans Snyder, Rubens's colleague and employee at his studio.

Rubens tackled this subject in two very similar versions. The Dresden version is now considered to have been the first, and as indisputably by the master's own hand. In a second version at the Hessisches Landesmuseum, Darmstadt, Rubens increased the format of the picture considerably; what previously had been a three-quarter-portrayal now became full-length, and the content was altered and enriched by the inclusion of additional figures.[1] The composition of the Darmstadt Diana inspired many more copies than the Dresden painting: apart from a study by Jacob Jordaens (Fitzwilliam Museum, Cambridge), three other versions are known, which must all be regarded as coming from Rubens's workshop. One was in Dresden until the end of the Second World War, but now numbers among the Gallery's war losses (former Gal. no. 980). UN

44

Anthony van Dyck (Antwerp 1599 – London 1641)
Portrait of a Man in Armour with Red Scarf, c.1625/27

Oil on canvas, 90 × 70 cm

Acquired in 1741 from the Wallenstein Collection in Dux

Gal. no. 1026

LITERATURE
Essen 1986, pp. 352ff., no. 474. Larsen 1988, vol. 2, p. 215, no. 532. Dresden 1992, p. 187.

NOTE
1 Dutch for 'little head'. Used to refer to character heads mostly shown in imaginative or exotic costumes, these became a popular motif in the Rembrandt school.

In October 1621, Anthony van Dyck left Antwerp for Italy. He reached Genoa by November, and was the guest of his fellow Flemings the de Wael brothers, who were art-dealers and painters. A number of extended journeys during his years in the peninsula up until 1627 took Van Dyck to all the main cities of northern and central Italy. He spent the majority of his time, however, in Genoa. Van Dyck's Italian period was strongly influenced by his intensive study of the masters of the Italian Renaissance, with the work of Titian leaving the deepest impression on him. He gained important inspiration, too, from the works of Veronese, Giorgione, Parmigianino and Carracci, among others, whose compositions he recorded on numerous occasions in his famous Italian sketchbook. Van Dyck made his mark in Italy as a portraitist, and numbered many important families from the upper strata of Genoese society among his clients.

It has yet to be clarified whether or not the *Portrait of a Man in Armour with Red Scarf* was one of these commissions; various attempts to identify the man in the picture have been inconclusive. The half-length portrait shows a young man with long hair wearing a dark suit of armour, who turns to the left and directs his gaze past the viewer. His right hand rests on a staff, while wrapped around the armour on his left arm is a red ribbon that has given rise to a great deal of speculation in the past. The young man's features are even, gentle and handsome, and lend him a proud yet questioning look. His black shiny armour with its silvery highlights, together with the vibrant colour contrast produced by the dark red bow, shows not only an elegance but also a great delicacy in the execution of the painting.

The question of the subject's identity recedes into the background when the picture is compared with another work by Van Dyck, also painted in 1625. The sole allegory that the artist painted during his years in Italy, *The Ages of Man* (Museo Civico d'Arte e Storia, Vicenza) was inspired by Titian's *Three Ages of Man* (c. 1512/15; on loan from the collection of the Duke of Sutherland to the National Gallery of Scotland, Edinburgh). In the work, Van Dyck's composition for the age of adulthood is represented by a pair of lovers. The young man at the centre of the picture is likewise shown half-length; his right hand rests on a staff; he wears a dark breastplate that strongly reflects the light; and wound about his shoulders and upper arm is a narrow strip of red cloth. Both his pose and the way his equipment is rendered are highly reminiscent of the Dresden *Portrait of a Man in Armour*. If the two paintings are linked, it seems likely that the Dresden work is likewise an allegory, in which case the subject's features would no longer be central to the painting's message, in much the same way, for instance, as with Dutch 'tronies'.[1] UN

45

Jacob Jordaens (Antwerp 1593 – Antwerp 1678)

Diana and Actaeon, *c.* 1640

Oil on oak panel,
53.5 × 75.5 cm

First entered in the
1722–28 inventory, A 1825,
as H. van Balen

Gal. no. 999

LITERATURE
Hulst 1966, p. 93, fig. 10.
Hulst 1982, p. 174, fig. 146.
Antwerp 1993, p. 194,
no. A 60.

NOTE
1 Ovid, *Metamorphoses*,
   Arthur Golding (trans.),
   1567, II, 184–85.

In the years around 1640, the successful Antwerp artist Jordaens painted a number of works with mythological scenes that differed strongly from his previous production, both in terms of dimensions and the relationship between figures and landscapes. The present work uses the Antwerp cabinet-painting format, a comparatively small size of picture for Jordaens that follows in the tradition of Frans Francken II, Hendrick van Balen and Jan Brueghel the Elder. *Diana and Actaeon* is the first example in Jordaens's *oeuvre* in which landscape came to assume an importance of its own, becoming as significant in the painting as the historical scene with its small-scale, almost incidental figures. This development was already apparent in Jordaens's 1635 painting *The Hunter and His Hounds* (Musée des Beaux-Arts, Lille) and reached its zenith some five years later in a number of idyllic landscapes enlivened by richly populated scenes from Greek mythology.

The painting in Dresden, depicting the meeting of Diana and Actaeon on the rocky banks of a stream, must be seen as one of the most important examples of this group. Fully in keeping with Ovid (*Metamorphoses*, III, 138–252), the hunter, who is on the left, carrying a spear and followed by his dogs, is dressed to great effect in a length of red cloth. Separated by no more than a narrow stretch of water flowing along the lower edge of the painting we see the naked figures of Diana and her companions, almost in a direct line before the hunter and seemingly lined up for the viewer. The blatant nudity of these delightful, voluptuous women departs strangely from Ovid's descriptions, in which, upon their discovery by Actaeon, the surprised nymphs try to cover and hide themselves.

In Jordaens's composition, Diana and her companions seem to have frozen somewhat half-heartedly into droll poses; after all, the depiction of the undraped female body was the major reason for the artist's choice of this subject. So Jordaens makes the most of his opportunity, and depicts the women caught performing their post-hunt ablutions in ten different positions, some curiously bent, some standing, and some crouching. With this group, whose prototypes sometimes reappear in his other mythological landscapes, Jordaens demonstrates his prowess in painting the nude. Characteristic figures, such as the standing woman protecting her virtue with her hand, the woman cowering to one side, or the nymph with one arm raised in fright, are very similarly depicted in *Diana and Callisto* (*c.* 1640, Private collection), for instance, or *Pan Punished by the Nymphs* (*c.* 1640, Mauritshuis, The Hague), or indeed twenty years earlier in the large-scale *Pan and Syrinx* (Koninklijke Musea voor Schone Kunsten, Brussels), which shows the fleeing Syrinx with one arm raised.

The landscape seems faithful to Ovid's description:

> Not made by hand nor man's devise, and yet no man alive,
> A trimmer piece of worke than that could for his life contrive.
> With flint and Pommy was it wallde by nature halfe about,
> And on the right side of the same full freshly flowed out
> A lively spring with Christall streame: whereof the upper brim
> Was greene with grasse and matted herbes that smelled verie trim.[1]

A grotto opens to the right beneath a rocky hill, from which Jordaens lets the spring flow forth and form a stream, taking the viewer's gaze with it deep into the picture. The group of trees in the shady zone of the foreground to the left simultaneously forms the frame for the flat river plain, and creates a compositional counterbalance to the dark form of the grotto and the ridge rising above. The dynamic landscape, with its bizarre broken tree trunk jabbing at the sky above the terrified nymph and its low-set horizon, is in the tradition of the Flemish forestscape, but does not match up to the works of Jordaens's fellow Antwerp artist Rubens. Jordaens, in whose *oeuvre* the landscape played but a marginal role, was nevertheless skilled in employing its elements to give weight to the content of figurative scenes and heighten drama. UN

46

David Teniers the Younger (Antwerp 1610 – Brussels 1690)
Kermis at the Half Moon Inn, 1641

Signed lower centre:
DAVID TENIERS F;
on the inn sign: 1641

Oil on canvas,
92.5 × 132 cm

1742, by de Brais from the
Carignan Collection, Paris

Gal. no. 1070

LITERATURE
Sacher 1981. Antwerp 1991,
no. 24.

NOTES
1 Antwerp 1991, no. 16.
2 Restoration work in 1980
surprisingly revealed that
the entire sky had been
overpainted by the Saxon
court painter Dietrich in
the eighteenth century
using thicker paint and
warmer hues. The
overpainting was removed
as part of the restoration
work; Sacher 1981.
3 Antwerp 1991, no. 12.
4 Tiegel-Hertfelder 1994,
pp. 34, 38ff.

Depictions of the 'kermis' or rural fair belong to an iconographic and compositional tradition founded in the Netherlands in about 1550 by Pieter Brueghel the Elder. So when David Teniers painted his first country fair in 1637,[1] his native town of Antwerp could already look back on an almost century-long tradition in this genre, meaning that as a 'kermisschilder' he was depicting a popular and successful subject. The Gemäldegalerie in Dresden owns two further works on the 'boerenkermis' by Teniers the Younger (Gal. nos 1081, 1083), and two other Flemish artists are represented with similar works, Hans Bol and David Vinckboons (Gal. nos 823, 937).

The *Kermis at the Half Moon Inn* shown here demonstrates how Teniers had grown away from Adriaen Brouwer and developed his own style, distinguished primarily by a lighter overall tone and warmer, more radiant colours. The scale of his figures is somewhat reduced in his village scenes, so that they fit more convincingly into his broad, expansive landscapes with their subtly shaded atmospheres. The festivities are being held here in a square, bounded on two sides by a wooden fence, in front of a village tavern similar to that in many other Flemish kermis paintings. This provides Teniers with the means to create a stage-like action space at the front that is divided from the surrounding deep space outside and above. A path leads off to the left in the direction of Antwerp Cathedral, which gives the rural festivities a local and municipal frame of reference. The sky, with its vivid stretches of cloud and the gold-tinged light of the evening on the left, is given a special weight,[2] which lends the scene a cool, airy atmosphere and a festive mood.

The joyful, lively antics of the farmers are not based on Teniers's own observations, but are pieced together from the handed-down repertoire of motifs for this genre, which were constantly varied and modified. They include the musicians standing on their podium, the three couples doing a round dance in the foreground, the drunk who is being helped home by two farmers, and the man who is leaning by the fence in an attack of nausea. At the end of the canvas on the right edge we also see the motif of the 'unequal couple': Teniers had already used lecherous old farmers hugging young girls as a single motif for a painting.[3] Also worthy of mention is the depiction within the painting of farming implements, arranged by the fence like a still-life; this device is often to be found in Teniers's work and reveals his artistic self-confidence. Not content with specialising in a single genre, he demands rather the special recognition of the connoisseur. A second scene on the right makes it clear how former, drastic depictions of 'gula' (greed in Latin) have here been diluted: a pig trots up to a sleeping farmer to give him a sniff. This motif can be traced back to Hans Sebald Beham (1539) and was also used by Adriaen Brouwer, but in their pictures the drunk lies on a bench being sick while a pig or a dog eats his vomit.[4] Teniers eliminates such representations and presents a more friendly and idyllic scene. Likewise there are no signs here of people attending to calls of nature.

This significant 'clean-up' of subject matter must be due to the collectors of these works, who were not keen to see rude displays of such deadly sins as gluttony and lust. The potential circle of buyers has even become part of the picture: at the left of the action, albeit as non-participant observers, we see a group of distinguished and elaborately dressed townsfolk. Arranged almost as if in a group portrait, and

with a stiff and measured air, they form the greatest conceivable contrast to the lively dancing farmers to their right. A potentially explosive attempt is being made to establish contact between the two groups: a farmer has taken a lady by the hand and invited her to dance, but he encounters resistance. His aim is to draw her from her safe position of observer into the actual swing of the kermis. The farmer's wife, suckling her child, watches suspiciously from a distance. This group of townsfolk can be interpreted as a reflexive break in the representation. Teniers refers to a conflict in the way such works are received: on the one hand there is the wish to join in by observing the carefree activities of simple farming folk, free of any responsibilities to etiquette. On the other, an urban bourgeoisie that takes the ideals of court life as its yardstick is unable to cross this boundary in person. The subject is charged because Teniers, as subsequent court painter and administrator of Archduke Albrecht's art collections, focuses in his views of the interior of the Archduke's galleries on the way his own country genre paintings are canonised when placed in the context of an aristocratic collection. A painting by Teniers in the Palace of Schleissheim steps over the social divide in exactly the opposite way: a farmer, flail in hand, looks very out of place as he poses in the royal gallery for the painter amid famous portraits and historical scenes. OK

47

Adriaen van Utrecht (Antwerp 1599 – Antwerp 1652/53)

Still-life with Hare and Birds on a Ring, second half of the 1640s

Signed lower centre on the table edge (falsely): J. Fyt. f.

Oil on canvas,
86 × 117 cm

Dresden inventory of 1754,
II, 88

Gal. no. 1215 A

LITERATURE
Greindl 1956, p.192. Dresden 1992, p.390. Vienna 2002, pp. 210ff.

NOTE
1 Robels 1989, cats 110, 111, 113, 121, 140, 141.

The Dresden *Still-life with Hare and Birds on a Ring* is one of a group of paintings that Van Utrecht produced in this form, beginning in the early 1640s, under the influence of small-format hunting pieces by Jan Fyt. A dead hare lies on a tabletop parallel to the painting's lower edge with its back legs trussed together, with a number of birds around an inverted wicker basket. An arrangement of vegetables, comprising a melon, cabbages and globe artichokes, balances them on the right-hand side. Suspended above the two groups is a ring hook, such is used for hanging game, to which five birds of differing sizes have been attached. The resulting pyramidal composition gives the still-life a greater tightness and more structure than many of Van Utrecht's other hunting pictures. The impression of spatial clarity is intensified by a number of small, cunningly used overlaps, which also produce a sense of depth.

A light source presumably located outside the painting to the left casts a strong narrow shaft of light onto the arrangement from the side. Some areas, such as the small birds skewered together on the rod at the front, remain in shadow. A softer light falls from the opposite side, a device that the painter used regularly to give body to the forms in his still-lifes.

The individual motifs in the Dresden painting demonstrate a precise knowledge of the creatures depicted, which interestingly consist solely of small game. A wild duck, hanging by one leg in a dominant central position, is framed by two kingfishers, a sparrow and a blackbird, all attached to the ring. The hare lying head down on the tabletop echoes the bird's vertical lines in its outstretched body and continues them in its two front legs hanging down at the front. Two dead snipe have been placed decoratively, although in a strange position, beside the hare, while a partridge leans against a basket. A bullfinch, a goldfinch, and a variety of other finches have been skewered on a rod that projects from the table, a visual idea that is echoed by the artichokes on the other side.

Adriaen van Utrecht drew inspiration in terms of both form and content from Frans Snyders, whose still-lifes with game and fowl[1] contain a number of comparable motifs. But the precision in Van Utrecht's painting, his constant attention to detail, and his controlled use of colour, centring chiefly on a cool grey with shades of brown, green and violet, is stylistically much closer to Jan Fyt.

The great interest shown by Van Utrecht's contemporaries in hunting still-lifes was no doubt partly due to the feudal hunting rights still in force during the seventeenth century, which granted the privilege to rulers and members of the nobility and the clergy. Hunting pieces were viewed as collections of trophies, and had a symbolic function for their owners as allegories of power over nature after it has succumbed in battle. The Dresden painting may equally have been seen in a quite different way: the contemporary viewer saw the still-life composed of animals and fruits as a portrayal of the richness of creation and as a symbol of its divine order. Some individual motifs might also have been understood as having their own special, often ambiguous, symbolism, such as the birds spread out on the table, which stood for earthly desire, or the artichokes, aphrodisiacs that awaken sexual craving. UN

48

Jacob Isaacksz van Ruisdael   (Haarlem 1628 or 1629 – Amsterdam 1682)
The Cloister, *c.* 1650/55

Signed lower right: JvR.
(interwoven)

Oil on canvas, 75 × 96 cm

First included in the 1754
inventory, II, 189

Gal. no. 1494

LITERATURE
Walford 1991, pp.84ff.,
fig. 77. Dresden 1992, p. 337,
no. 1492. Frankfurt 1994,
pp. 20–22, no. 3. Slive 2001,
no. 535. Weimar 2002,
pp. 247ff., under no. 171.

NOTES
1 *Ruysdael als Dichter*, 1806,
   cf. Goethes Werke,
   Weimar Ausgabe I, 48,
   pp. 164–66.
2 Nicolaes Berchem,
   *Landscape with Bentheim
   Castle* (Gal. no. 1481);
   Jacob Isaacksz van
   Ruisdael, *The Castle at
   Bentheim* (Gal. no. 1496).

Johann Wolfgang von Goethe always stopped to admire Ruisdael's landscapes during his visits to the Dresden Gemäldegalerie in 1768, 1790 and 1794. He regarded them as the incarnation of an ideal landscape that corresponded to his own classical aesthetic. Goethe first began to develop his thoughts on art theory in 1813 in his text 'Über das Ruysdaelische Kloster', which was later to become the key essay in his trilogy of works *Ruysdael als Dichter*. Goethe's texts clearly reveal his anti-Romantic sentiments and were rightly regarded as an affront to the new art of the Romantics, especially that of Caspar David Friedrich. Goethe compared their work with that of Ruisdael, a form of painting that employed similar motifs during the creative process to achieve an idealised heightening and transformation of the subject. 'The second painting, renowned under the name *The Cloister*, is aimed at depicting things past in the present, which has been achieved in the most admirable manner, bringing the quick and the dead into most vivid communication…The picture has been taken from nature in the most felicitous way, and heightened equally by ideation, and since moreover it has been laid out and executed to meet every demand of art, it will never fail to exert an attraction on us',[1] as Goethe wrote in 1816 on the Dresden *Cloister*, which evidently fitted very well with his thoughts on art theory and aesthetics.

Painted around the mid-1650s, *The Cloister* is one of a group of works directly influenced by Ruisdael's travels around the German-Netherlandish borderlands, the regions of Overijssel and Westphalia. Together with his friend and fellow painter Nicolaes Berchem (1620–1683), Ruisdael set out in 1650 on a hike to Burgsteinfurt, which took the two painters through Bentheim. The castle there was to become an important motif to both artists in a number of drawings and paintings executed right into the middle of the decade.[2] But of more importance to Ruisdael's overall development was the impression he gained from the landscapes he traversed, even if their appearance in his pictures can rarely be pinned down with any certainty. Consequently, the distinct change in his style, the new, prevailing 'romantic' mood in the works of this period, has been ascribed to Ruisdael's encounters with nature during his journey.

The Dresden *Cloister* unites a number of painterly and compositional elements that clearly relate directly to Ruisdael's impressions from his journey: the open, generously composed riverscape contains a number of 'non-Dutch' motifs, such as a cloister complex with a ruined tower on the riverbank, the dark, overgrown hill ridge in the background, and the bizarrely shaped, knotty trunks of the ancient trees on the right-hand side of the picture. The pale bark of the dead tree on the right-hand riverbank corresponds to the ochre façade of the ruins, warmly lit by the evening sun. Dark, heavy clouds gather over the hills against the pale evening sky, whose light is reflected by flat areas of the riverbank. The careful, finely detailed work on the foliage, the pure, cool coloration, and the richer and more powerful approach of this picture go far beyond Ruisdael's works from the 1640s.

The artist sketching scenery in the foreground of the Dresden *Cloister* invites the viewer to immerse himself in contemplation at the sight of the genesis and decay of nature and of the achievements of civilisation. This is totally in keeping with Carel van Mander's engraving *The Transience of Human Life*, published in 1599, in which the life of man is compared with a tree and with flowing water. UN

149

49

Philips Wouwerman (Haarlem 1619 – Haarlem 1668)

Setting Out on the Hunt, *c.* 1660/65

Signed lower left: Phils. W.

Oil on oak panel, 45 × 64 cm

Purchased in 1755 from the estate of Pasquier in Paris, previously owned by Chevalier d'Orléans and in the art cabinet of Vicomte Angran de Fontpertuis; first appearance in the Dresden catalogue, 1765, Galerie Extérieure no. 243

Gal. no. 1439

LITERATURE
Schumacher 1989. Bürger 2001. Dijon 2001, no. 54. Hamburg 2002, no. 30.

This painting and its pendant (illustrated below) number among Wouwerman's later works. They date from a period in which his attention was chiefly devoted to hunting scenes. Indeed, about two hundred paintings on this theme are known from his hand.

Hunting was one of the favourite pastimes of the country nobility during the seventeenth century. Elegant hunting scenes appealed to aristocratic art collectors who were able to identify with them and saw their rank and prestige reflected in them. With a number of variations in subject matter, it was possible to cater for a great diversity of tastes. But apart from subject matter, artistic execution was also of importance to the collectors: the richness of the detailing in Wouwerman's paintings, the careful reproduction of the scenes, his fine, precise brush strokes, as well as his sensitive and subtle depiction of people and animals, all were especially valued by art lovers in the seventeenth and eighteenth centuries.

In *Setting Out on the Hunt* the horses have been saddled and the hounds are waiting in front of a grand country house for the chase to begin. The scene is aristocratic in character, as can be seen not only from the noble villa, but also from the sculptures adorning the buildings, the Baroque fountain, and the elegance of the hunting party. Wouwerman introduces a touch of genre painting into the work by placing a mother with two children squatting on the ground and a beggar asking for alms to the left of the picture.

In the pendant, *Return from the Hunt*, the young mistress of the house and a maid stand on the steps awaiting the party's return. A hunter approaches from the left leading a donkey loaded with game; a stag lies in the middleground with a couple of hounds. While grooms unhitch the horses or tend to the hounds, a huntsman presents the lady with a hare. This allusion to love was doubtless understood at the time. This motif, together with the Bacchus Fountain to the left of the steps, allows a moralising streak to be surmised. Bacchus stands for intemperate drinking that triggers high spirits and foolhardiness, and entices people to stray down the thorny path of bawdiness, gambling or song.

The elegant subject matter, the expansive southern landscape, the horses caught most faithfully in their movements, the depictions of figures with loving attention to detail, and the sensitive use of colour are all typical of Wouwerman's late period. These characteristics suggest that the works were painted in the 1660s, a dating that is further upheld by the style of the figures' clothing. KB/DW

Return from th

Oil on oa.
45.5 × 64 cm. Ga

50

Gabriel Metsu (Leiden 1629 – Amsterdam 1667)

Portrait of the Artist with His Wife Isabella de Wolff in a Tavern, 1661

Signed upper left:
G. Metsu 1661

Oil on oak panel,
35.5 × 30.5 cm

Gift prior to 1711 from the
Wackerbarth Collection,
inventory 1722–28, A 551

Gal. no. 1732

LITERATURE
Renckens and Duyvetter
1959. Robinson 1974, pp. 29,
32, 64, 78ff., fig. 34. Dresden
1992, p. 265. Dresden 2000A,
pp. 53ff.

NOTES
1 Renckens and Duyvetter
  1959, pp. 179–81, figs 2, 3.
2 Renckens and Duyvetter
  1959, p. 182.

The Dresden *Portrait of the Artist with His Wife* was for many years known simply as 'The Lovers at Breakfast'. Dressed in their finery the couple sit side by side in a room, which is revealed by numerous items and the woman at the blackboard to be in a tavern. The man and his wife are illuminated by an unseen light source from the front left. The man is laughing and puts his left arm around the young woman's shoulders, a gesture echoed by her arm as she hands him some berries. He raises a flute glass in his right hand to her health, while she looks straight ahead rather stiffly. Beside the couple a table is laid with a silver pot, some dried fish and a small loaf of bread, but the way it has been truncated at one end gives it the look of a stage prop. The rear of the tavern is in shadow, so that all that may be distinguished is the incidental figure chalking up orders in front of the fireplace, a narrow shelf, and an empty birdcage hanging above. The room opens up to the rear at the right, giving a view of a sunny courtyard in which a market stall has been erected.

The two protagonists, quite different in type, have been identified as the artist and Isabella de Wolff, whom he married in 1658 and who was a niece of the painter Pieter de Grebber. A comparison between the couple shown here and two small portraits of the artist and his wife, now in the keeping of the Speed Art Museum in Louisville, Kentucky, has confirmed that the Dresden work is indeed a self-portrait.[1] Particularly striking is the contrast between the artist's highly fashionable garments and the dark, high-necked outfit worn by his wife, the local costume of the region of Enkhuizen, although it was also worn in other parts of Holland. Isabella's hairstyle is curious, because normally this kind of braided coif is worn only by unmarried women.[2] The same Enkhuizen costume is also worn by the woman in *Young Couple Eating Breakfast* (Staatliche Kunsthalle Karlsruhe), a work painted by Metsu in 1667 which is similar in motif and composition to the double portrait in Dresden.

In paintings such as this, Metsu demonstrated, some four years after moving to Amsterdam, that he was at the height of his creative powers. Although in his younger years he had been interested in historical painting, he now concentrated mainly on intimate figurative works in private, domestic settings. At times the composition of these paintings is weighed down by too much narrative detail, but at others – as here – it is clear and crisp. Metsu's fairly relaxed and broad brushwork from this period shows no more than a trace of the Feinmaler style. Yet he was still able to reproduce leather, glass or metal with enormous sensitivity and delicacy.

The iconography of the painting distinguishes it as part of a painting tradition well-known to the educated contemporary viewer: the carousing, feasting couple, the ambience of the tavern with the landlady at the blackboard, the highly significant bread and fish still-life on the table. All of these elements point to the subject of the 'prodigal son regaling with the harlots in the inn'. This Biblical parable, much loved and widespread in seventeenth-century Dutch painting, was understood as an admonition against a life of sin and vice. A link between the Biblical story and an artist's self-portrait was not, however, completely unusual. Rembrandt, for instance, had depicted himself in a similar pose some twenty years earlier, in his *Self portrait with Saskia in the Scene from the Prodigal Son*, which is also in the Dresden collection (Gal. no. 1559). UN

51–52

Gabriel Metsu (Leiden 1629 – Amsterdam 1667)

The Poultry Seller, 1662
The Poultry Woman, 1662

The Poultry Seller, 1662
Signed left beneath the
centre of the window:
G. Metsu. 1662

Oil on oak panel,
61.5 × 45.7 cm

Inventory 1722–28, A 558,
at the auction by Jacob
Cromhout and Caspar
Loskart in Amsterdam
on 7 May 1709, no. 14, for
4,000 fl.; gift prior to 1711
through Wackerbarth

Gal. no. 1733

The Poultry Woman, 1662
Signed upper right on the
white notice: G Metsu 1662

Oil on oak panel,
61 × 45.2 cm

Inventory 1722–28, A 696,
purchased 1710 by Court
Commissioner Raschke
at Jacques de Witt, art-
dealers, in Amsterdam
for 150 pistoles

Gal. no. 1734

LITERATURE
Jongh 1968–69, pp. 22–52.
Amsterdam 1976, pp. 166–69.
Dresden 1992, pp. 265ff.
Dresden 2000A, pp. 57ff.

NOTES
1 Dresden 2000A, pp. 10ff.
2 Robinson 1974, p. 53,
  compares the saleswoman
  with the woman in
  Terborch's *Greeting*.
3 Jongh 1968–69, pp. 22ff.;
  Amsterdam 1976, pp.
  166ff.; Dresden 2000A,
  pp. 57ff.

Despite Leiden being his birthplace, Gabriel Metsu is not regarded as one of the city's 'Feinmaler', as a result of the great variations in the style and quality of his work. Nevertheless, these two paintings should be viewed in the same context as the 'fijnschilders'. This connection is all the more plausible when it is remembered that Augustus the Strong had a policy of buying the works of the Leiden Feinmaler:[1] the majority of Dresden's small Dutch wooden panels were acquired between 1708 and 1711, including the two works exhibited here. Like the other Feinmaler paintings, they were kept until 1806 in the private chambers of the royal palace, which testifies to the great esteem in which they were held. Augustus the Strong's attention must have been particularly drawn to Metsu's late paintings, for it was not until the late 1650s that his work became close to that of the Feinmalers; Metsu's paintings from the early 1660s, especially the two in Dresden, constitute a high point in his dialogue with the School and simultaneously of his creative output as a whole.

Market and kitchen scenes originally came from Flemish painting and above all are linked in the sixteenth century with Pieter Aertsen and Joachim Beuckelaer. In sharp contrast to Dutch still-life specialists, the Leiden Feinmalers around Gerard Dou reactivated these subjects for their small-format genre paintings, in which market goods were showed off to their best advantage in small, select groups. Metsu's *Poultry Seller* depicts just such a group of varied items, arranged along the painting's lower and left-hand margins; the precision with which they have been painted testifies to a supreme virtuosity in the Feinmaler style, and is accentuated in part by the use of light and dark contrasts. But importantly, each surface receives the same amount of attention: from different woods – a bamboo rod, basketwork, a barrel and a bare tree – to the fluffy fur of the rabbit beside the pale flesh of the plucked hen in the basket, or from the bird's skeletal head, a strong contrast with the luminous red head of the turkey, to the trader's thick wool stockings that differ so from his young customer's delicate, filmy gauze apron. Metsu is not simply content, however, to use the Feinmalers' technique of applying flat, narrow brush strokes one beside the next. The tree and the row of houses in the background reveal his command of a far more relaxed and expansive style. Furthermore, his colours are richer than those of the Leiden Feinmaler, and reveal a love of clear reds, blues and greens demonstrated, for instance, in the young woman's clothes. It has been suggested in this context that Metsu found inspiration for this distinguished-looking figure in Terborch's celebrated depictions of women.[2]

Although the two Metsus were not purchased together and the number of figures differs, the works can be regarded as pendants. They are identical in size, bear the same date, show the same motif using variously a male or a female protagonist, are set in the one case in a town and in the other in a village, and reveal a number of elements in common: in both cases an old man with one exposed knee sits beneath a bare tree with long branches that extend from the painting's edge to its centre; and both paintings depict an inquisitive little spaniel, as well as plants painted with botanical precision in their respective lower inside corners.

The *Poultry Seller* assumed importance for the interpretation of Dutch painting because Eddie de Jongh (1968/69) developed his ideas on 'Erotica in Vogelperspectief' (erotica from a bird's-eye view) chiefly on the basis of this work. With it he made an important contribution to an iconographic approach that left

an indelible mark on the analysis of Dutch art during the 1970s and 1980s.[3] Following this theory, depictions of birdcages or of people buying birds have assumed an overtly sexual connotation for the contemporary viewer, for the Netherlands word 'vogelen' (bird-catching) was a widespread colloquialism for sexual congress. On a second level, a bird-seller, a 'vogelaar', demonstrates his potency to the young woman with the live hen and makes obscene advances towards her as a 'hennetaster' (a chicken-feeler, who detects whether a hen is about to lay eggs). A similar wealth of innuendo is to be found in the *Poultry Woman*, in which we see an empty, open birdcage and two people haggling over a dead, plucked chicken. The chicken is being sold, moreover, by a young woman to an old lady, while the dealer looks on quite disinterestedly. Old women are often used in Dutch paintings as models of Christian virtue and the fear of God. In contrast to the *Poultry Seller*, the *Poultry Woman* might be showing an exchange of goods without any sexual allusions, or perhaps making reference to a romantic relationship that has come to an end.

Aside from this symbolism, it is worth asking whether by painting a market scene in which goods are being offered, scrutinised and exchanged, Metsu is trying to make an offer of his own to the viewer. In that case this rich and manifold 'visual overture' would be his attempt to convince the potential buyer of the quality of his own goods: his paintings. OK

53
Nicolaes Pietersz Berchem (Haarlem 1620 – Amsterdam 1683)
Herdsmen and Herds at a Waterfall, *c.* 1665

Signed left on the cliff:
N Berchem

Oil on canvas,
110 × 153 cm

Acquired after 1749 by
Le Leu from the collection
of the copper-etcher
J. A. Crozat, Paris; first
appearance in the Dresden
catalogue 1765, cat. no. 151

Gal. no. 1486

LITERATURE
Schaar 1958, pp.82ff. Mexico
1980, no. 5. Dijon 2001, no.
46. Hamburg 2002, no. 32.

Nicolaes Berchem, son of the still-life painter Pieter Claesz, belongs to the second generation of Netherlandish Italianists. As yet, no reliable sources are known to exist about a possible visit he may have made to Italy. The only indication of this that we have is a sudden change in style in 1653, which might have been triggered by new impressions from the south. Since Berchem can be shown to have been back in Haarlem by 1656, his Italian journey would most likely have taken place in the years between 1653 and 1655.

The Dresden landscape *Herdsmen and Herds at a Waterfall* was not, however, painted until the 1660s, during a phase of the artist's production which occurred long after any Italian journey. The work shows a rocky valley with a mountain river running through it whose source appears to be the waterfall in the distance. The steep wooded riverbank to the left faces a craggy cliff face on the other side. A couple of goatherds rest on the rocky plateau below, while a larger herd of cattle is being driven off to the right. A narrow path on the far right leads down to the water. A number of other sheep and cattle are being driven along this bank, to cross the river at a shallow spot. The eye moves from the lower edge of the picture up the valley and into the distance, towards sunny mountain uplands. The very painterly emphasis on individual motifs in the foreground, such as the naked branch lying partly in the water, the vegetation on the bank, and the trunks of the large trees, partly denuded of their bark, is characteristic of Berchem's style from around 1660 onwards. The bright light in the foreground and the bold shadows it casts make the details of the vegetation and rocky landscape stand out clearly. By contrast, the middleground and background are bathed in a soft, diffuse light and seem to swim before our eyes. The use of harsh light and the sharpness of the contours of the individual motifs reveal the influence of Adam Pijnacker on Berchem's later work. The Dresden painting, in an unusually large format for Berchem, can be regarded as a typical example of this influence. UN

The
Spanish
School

54

Diego Rodríguez de Silva y Velázquez (Seville 1599 – Madrid 1660)

Juan Mateos, shortly before 1634

Oil on canvas,
109.3 × 90.4 cm;
original canvas
106 × 87 cm

Mentioned 1685 in the
inventory of the estate
of Cesare Ignazio d'Este;
1746 from the Ducal Gallery
in Modena

Gal. no. 697

LITERATURE
Inv. Dresden 1754, no. A 480.
Riedel and Wenzel 1765,
pp. 105ff., no. A 531. Riedel
1801, p. 77, no. A 530.
Dresden Cat. 1838, p. 175,
no. J 57. Dresden Cat. 1848,
p. 75, no. J 637. Justi 1903,
pp. 342ff. Posse 1929, p. 343.
Posse 1930, p. 220. Brown
1986, pp. 144ff. Dresden 1992,
p. 393. López-Rey 1996A,
no. 58. Brown, in Madrid
1999, no. 22.

NOTES
1 López-Rey 1996A, no. 57.
2 Detail in López-Rey
  1996B, p. 90.
3 López-Rey 1996A, no. 76.

A brilliant conjecture from Carl Justi gave new direction to research into the largest and most important Velázquez portrait in Dresden. Justi was struck by the similarity between the sitter and the portrait of Juan Mateos, the Royal Master of the Hunt, on the frontispiece of Mateos's treatise on the origins and dignity of the hunt, published in 1634 by Francisco Martínez. The dimensions and intentions of the two works defy every comparison, but agreements in the alignment of the man's upper body and his head, his exceptionally short hair, the ear, the chin and, not least, the penetrating gaze directed at the viewer, make it more than tempting to follow Justi. As for the sitter's clothing, the engraving, although generally quite unspecific, repeats the tight row of buttons on the man's chest, strengthening the impression that the Dresden portrait formed the basis for the engraving. The hunt may also be indicated by the heavy gloves in the painting, previously misinterpreted as roughly sketched hands, and the revolver – even if it can only be surmised – that the man seems to reach for with his right hand. Mateos died in 1643, and from 1641 to 1643 Ippolito Camillo Guidi was in Madrid searching for paintings while serving as Modenese ambassador. The painting can first be identified certainly with the date of June 1685 in the inventory of Prince Cesaro Ignazio d'Este.

If we follow it, Justi's conjecture allows an advance in three aspects of our knowledge of Velázquez. It leads to the identification of a portrait of someone other than a member of the royal family, their Minister Olivares (Gal. no. 699), or to the dwarves and fools who populated the palace. It gives us an insight into the levels of society that other sitters might be expected to come from, perhaps unsurprisingly the elevated courtiers. And finally and above all else, it provides clues for research into Velázquez's *oeuvre*, whose dating is still very uncertain.

The latest possible date, shortly before the publication of the treatise, would still be very early – scarcely more than three years after Velázquez's Italian journey, which brought about a fundamental change in his work, and immediately before the period in which he painted the *Surrender of Breda* (Museo del Prado, Madrid). In that case, we are witnessing here the painter's mature style, almost perfectly developed, over a quarter of a century before his death. The ground was applied in irregular patches using a spatula, in a manner typical of the artist; the picture is painted thinly, and the clothes, revolver and facial details are indicated with great economy.

And indeed, the painterly side of the work also seems to provide confirmation of the sitter's identity. Although it would mean a very large step forward in his development compared, say, to the portrait in Fort Worth,[1] its closeness to portraits of the royal family reliably dated between 1632 and 1635 is seductive, especially in the milky reflections that shimmer on the sitters' skin.[2] However, the distance from the portrait of the sculptor Martínez Montañés,[3] certainly done in 1635/36 and to which the Dresden portrait has the most outward resemblance, is considerable.

The two lengths of canvas that were appended to the right from the beginning demonstrate how careless Velázquez was about such extraneous details.

Even before its purchase by Dresden, attributions wavered between Velázquez and Rubens. The painting is ascribed in the Dresden catalogues not only to Rubens (1765, 1801), but also to Titian (1817–38), before appearing once again in 1848 as a work by Velázquez. Particularly remarkable is the attribution in the inventory of 1754, where it is described as an anonymous 'Portrait eines Grand d'Espagne'. MW

55

Diego Rodríguez de Silva y Velázquez (Seville 1599 – Madrid 1660)

Portrait of a Knight of the Order of Santiago, *c.* 1635 or after

Oil on canvas, 67.3 × 56 cm

1685 in the possession of Prince Cesare Ignazio d'Este of Modena; 1746 from the Ducal Gallery in Modena to Dresden

Gal. no. 698

LITERATURE
Inv. Dresden 1754, no. 559. Riedel and Wenzel 1765, p. 72, no. A 368. Dresden Cat. 1826, p.35, no. A 207. Matthäi 1837, p.197, no. A 1000. Dresden Cat. 1853, p. 17, no. A 109a. Posse 1929, p. 343. Posse 1930, p.220. Dresden 1992, p.394. Madrid 1999. Rome 2001, pp. 250ff. Hamburg 2002, no. 20.

NOTE
1 Justi 1903, vol. 2, p.97.

Among the hundred best paintings of the Este collection purchased from Modena by Augustus III were three works by Diego Velázquez. On their arrival in Dresden in 1746, and for over a century afterwards, these majors works were, with the exception of a portrait of a young nobleman in Munich, the only paintings by the artist in Germany.

Now regarded as the master of Spanish painting, Velázquez – unlike Murillo and Ribera – was virtually unknown outside his native country during the eighteenth century; even today half of the some hundred works known to be by his own hand are still in Spain.

Thus it is scarcely surprising that the portrait was treated at the time of its purchase as a work by Peter Paul Rubens, even though the inventory of Prince Cesare Ignazio d'Este had described it correctly in 1685 as an original by Velázquez. The catalogues of the Gemäldegalerie continued for the next century to refer to the painting as either by Rubens or his pupil Van Dyck; not until 1853 was the correct attribution given. The mistaken attribution can help us to gain a better understanding of the painting (which research until now has clearly dated too late). Rubens spent nine months in 1628/29 in Madrid, and Velázquez's meeting with the great man of Flemish painting gave a decisive impetus to the young Spaniard's artistic development. And although presumably he never knew him in person, Velázquez was able to study Van Dyck's paintings – and to match his own prowess against them, as he evidently liked to do – in Italy and also in the royal collection in Madrid, for which he was partly responsible as court painter. Through their close study of Titian, the naturalness of their approach, the immediacy of their portrayals, and their depth of psychological penetration, the portraits of the mature Velázquez come far closer to Van Dyck than to any of his Spanish contemporaries. The parallels extend even to the thin, almost sketchy manner in which the two artists applied their paint.

The man's hair hangs over his ears like a veil, and Velázquez has deliberately incorporated the ground here as part of the effect. He is content with economical strokes, dashed off lightly but with the utmost confidence, to indicate the details of the garments. The few corrections he makes are not difficult to detect with the naked eye. This technique is frequently encountered in Velázquez's works, preventing us from agreeing with Carl Justi, the great German researcher of Spanish art, when he says that the Dresden portrait reveals 'through its unfinished state the artist at work'.[1]

Even the one indication of the sitter's identity, the red cross of the Knights of the Order of Santiago, is painted so hazily that it was only first correctly identified about one hundred years ago. It is interesting to note, through, that the sitter was already regarded in the eighteenth century as a Spaniard. MW

56
Jusepe de Ribera (Xátiva 1591 – Naples 1652)
Diogenes, 1637

Signed right: Jusepe de Ribera español, F. 1637

Oil on canvas, 76 × 61 cm

First mentioned in the 1722–28 inventory; according to which delivered by Baron Schacht

Gal. no. 682

LITERATURE
Inv. Dresden 1722–28, f. 6, no. [A] 250. Inv. Dresden 1754, no. J 214. Riedel and Wenzel 1765, no. J.87. Lehninger 1782, p.193, no. J.87. Posse 1929, p.338. McFadyen Felton 1971, no. S-31. Pérez Sánchez and Spinosa 1978, no. 110; Dresden 1992, p.318. New York 1992, no. 43.

NOTE
1 Paris 1990, pp.206–08.

Of all the Dresden works currently ascribed to the Spanish School, *Diogenes* has resided the longest in the Gemäldegalerie. It is also the one painting associated with the name Jusepe de Ribera that is undisputedly by the artist's own hand. Although they have been reinforced in later restoration work, the signature and date are also quite certainly Ribera's own. The esteem in which the painting was held during the eighteenth century is shown by the fact that it was one of the paintings selected for the so-called *Galeriewerk*, a compendium of engravings taken from works in the Gemäldegalerie. The number it received in the 1722 inventory has remained to this day in the lower-right corner of the painting.

The most famous of the Cynics, the philosopher Diogenes of Sinope, who died in 323 BC, is provided here with a lamp by way of an attribute. According to his own statement, he used it in broad daylight to find a 'genuine person' on a bustling marketplace – a subject that Jacob Jordaens was to capture with great eloquence and opulence five years after Ribera in a painting that is likewise one of the highlights of the Gemäldegalerie (Gal. no. 1010). The subject was much loved throughout Baroque Europe, although it appears that the Italians preferred to depict the philosopher alone, as with this and another painting by Ribera, while the densely populated scenes preferred by Jordaens were more popular in the Netherlands.

Ribera was interested in studying different types of people, and even his religious paintings seem to be populated with figures taken from the everyday world about him, in the tradition of Caravaggio. The subject of this portrait must have prompted this depiction of an eccentric outsider, his hair tangled, his beard unkempt, his hands work-worn, dressed in simple apparel, and directing a penetrating gaze at the beholder. The great Cynic's stare led as early as 1782 to Lehninger's somewhat ridiculed surmise that the artist had depicted himself in this painting.

A study of the work gives a very impressive insight into the speed, grace and supreme confidence with which the mature Ribera defined his forms. X-rays have revealed that in comparison to his earlier works, he reduced the thickness of the individual layers of paint by an appreciable amount. Many of the effects were created by reworking the ground while it was still wet. The format is unusual: Ribera chose an oval picture field, although the canvas itself is rectangular. This approach is unique in his *oeuvre*, although it is to be found among various of his contemporaries, above all among the Netherlanders, but also in the works of Ribera's Neapolitan colleagues Francesco Fracanzano and Simon Vouet. In 1621 Vouet, who like Ribera had previously spent many years in Rome, painted one of the Dorias in Genoa, a portrait that has resided since 1979 in the Louvre. The artist kept the portrait, perhaps originally conceived as rectangular, to an oval, and in this it resembles a very similar Doria portrait by Vouet that exists as an engraving.[1] In the cases of both Vouet and Ribera, this format may indicate that the painting was designed to fit the wall décor in the house of a nobleman.

Ribera regularly denotes himself as a Spaniard in his signature. Although his career as a painter developed almost entirely in Italy, first in Rome, then in Naples, it should not be forgotten that at that time, Naples belonged to Spain and was ruled over by Spanish viceroys – who numbered among Ribera's most important clients – even though the majority of its inhabitants and of his fellow painters were Italian. MW

57
Bartolomé Esteban Murillo (Seville 1617 – Seville 1682)
Mary with Child, *c. 1670/80*

Oil on canvas,
166 × 115 cm

Purchased in 1755 at the
auction of the Pasquier
Collection, Paris

Gal. no. 705

LITERATURE
Riedel and Wenzel 1765,
p. 143, no. A.726. Lehninger
1782, p. 216, no. A.726.
Dresden Cat. 1843, p. 18,
Gal. A.110. Matthäi 1837,
p. 107, Gal. J.539. Schäfer
1860, pp. 1285–88, no. 607.
Posse 1929, pp. 347ff. Posse
1930, p. 141. Angulo Íñiguez
1981, no. 147. Dresden 1992,
p. 275.

NOTE
1 Xanthe Brooke, in London
2001, pp. 55ff.

The Dresden Madonna is a particularly beautiful work from Murillo's late period. Over the decades, Murillo's painting became increasingly delicate and gossamer-like as the boundaries between his forms progressively dissolved. In this last phase of his creative production, he applies paint so thinly in places that the structure of the underpainting can clearly be seen. The white of the swaddling clothes has been given more strength, although the painter was not concerned here about creating a unified surface and simply placed one brush stroke directly beside the next. A delicate hint of pink shimmers on the Virgin's cheeks, and the pink of her fingers makes them stand out from the more pallid flesh tones of the infant Jesus. The subject has been reduced to its essence and the colours restricted to a few basic tones, although the effect of Mary's cloak has been spoilt by the changes that take place in blue pigments over time. The neutral background and the child's gaze, which appears to have moved spontaneously from its mother to a visitor who has suddenly entered, heighten the work's sense of intimacy. Not without reason does the description in the catalogues from 1817 to 1844 – 'Portrait of a mother with her gaze turned to heaven, holding her child on her lap' prompt us to ask whether anyone at that time was still aware of the picture's true subject.

The painting was acquired in 1755, directly before the outbreak of the Seven Years War put an abrupt end to Dresden's glorious years of collecting. With its flowing forms, its cool but harmonious use of colour, and the noble, charming yet demure features of the mother and child, it made a perfect addition to the Dresden collection of works by Van Dyck and above all Rubens, whose paintings were an inspiration for Murillo whenever they found their way to Spain. Indeed, the Madonna was placed in the old gallery building alongside the paintings of the northern schools. She hung there in 1765 with numerous works of the Rembrandt and Rubens schools, and from some time before 1801 until after 1833 among a group of works by Adriaen van der Werff and other Netherlanders, beneath Jacob Jordaens's *The Presentation in the Temple* (Gal. no. 1012). Not until after this was a small group of Spanish paintings put together and hung in the rooms otherwise set apart for Italian painting. In 1855 the picture, with a large number of new acquisitions, was moved to the large Spanish room in the new building.

It is instructive that the painting was not acquired in Spain, but, as with many of the collection's key pictures by Rubens or Rembrandt, in Paris. Johann August Lehninger tells us in 1782 that Murillo's works were in demand all over Europe, and indeed unlike other Spanish artists – the one exception being Ribera, who had adopted Naples as his home – he was avidly collected during his own lifetime. Whereas Velázquez was only first 'discovered' during the course of the nineteenth century, and El Greco not before 1900, copies of Murillo's works were already being made in Antwerp decades before his death. They made their way to England shortly after, alongside originals by his own hand.[1]

Murillo's Madonna was pierced by several bullets during the revolutionary unrest of May 1849. X-rays and the circular craquelure around the bullet holes confirm that these reports should not be dismissed as mere legends. The holes, which immediately afterwards were patched and retouched, are at the end of Mary's right thumb, to the left above her headscarf, and to the left in the background. The painting's present state is due to restoration work carried out in 1970. MW

Bibliography

Adhémar 1950
Hélène Adhémar, *Watteau: sa vie, son oeuvre*, Paris, 1950

Agueda Villar 1991
Mercedes Agueda Villar, 'Una colección de pinturas en el Madrid del siglo XVIII. El Marqués de la Ensenada', in *Cinco siglos de arte en Madrid (15–20)*, 3, *Jornadas de Arte*, Madrid, CSIC, 1991, pp. 165–77

Akinscha and Koslow 1995
Konstantin Akinscha and Grigori Koslow, *Beutekunst. Auf Schatzsuche in russischen Geheimdepots*, Munich, 1995

Amsterdam 1976
Tot Lering en Vermaak. Betekenissen van Hollandse genrevorstellingen uit de zeventiende eeuw, exh. cat., Rijksmuseum, Amsterdam, 1976

Amsterdam 1999
Rembrandt's Treasures, Bob van den Boogert (ed.), exh. cat., Rembrandthuis, Amsterdam, 1999–2000

Andrews 1985
Keith Andrews, *Adam Elsheimer. Werkverzeichnis der Gemälde, Zeichnungen und Radierungen*, Munich, 1985

Angulo Íñiguez 1981
Diego Angulo Íñiguez, *Murillo*, Madrid, 1981

Antwerp 1977
Peter Paul Rubens. Paintings, Oil Sketches, Drawings, exh. cat., Koninklijk Museum voor Schone Kunsten, Antwerp, 1977

Antwerp 1991
David Teniers de Jonge. Schilderijen, Tekeningen, Margret Klinge (ed.), exh. cat., Koninklijk Museum voor Schone Kunsten, Antwerp, 1991

Antwerp 1993
Jacob Jordaens (1593–1678), Hans Devisscher and Nora de Poorter (eds), exh. cat., Koninklijk Museum voor Schone Kunsten, 3 vols, Antwerp, 1993

Anzelewsky 1991
Fedja Anzelewsky, *Albrecht Dürer. Das malerische Werk*, new edition, Berlin, 1991

Aragon and Cocteau 1957
Louis Aragon and Jean Cocteau, *Entretiens sur le musée de Dresde*, Paris, 1957

Argenville 1762
Antoine Joseph Dezallier d'Argenville, *Abrégé de la vie des plus fameux peintres, avec leurs portraits gravés…*, Paris, 1762

Argenville 1768
Antoine Joseph Dezallier d'Argenville, *Abrégé de la vie des plus fameux peintres*, 2 vols, Paris, 1745; German edition, Leipzig, 1767–68; vol. 4, 1768

Asche 1961
S. Asche, *Drei Bildhauerfamilien an der Elbe*, Vienna and Wiesbaden, 1961

Badt 1969
Kurt Badt, *Die Kunst des Nicolas Poussin*, 2 vols, Cologne, 1969

Bagnol 1988
Eliane Bagnol, *Christian Wilhelm Ernst Dietrich. Etat de travaux et recensement de l'oeuvre (mémoire de D. E. A.)*, Université Paul-Valéry, Montpellier III, 1988

Baldissin Molli 1994
Giovanna Baldissin Molli, 'Note biografiche su alcuni artisti veronesi del Settecento', *Bolletino del Museo Civico di Padova*, 83, 1994, pp. 131–68

Bang 1987
Marie Lødrop Bang, *Johan Christian Dahl 1788–1857. Life and Works*, 3 vols, Oslo, 1987

Bätschmann and Griener 1997
Oskar Bätschmann and Pascal Griener, *Hans Holbein*, Cologne, 1997

Bellonci and Garavaglia 1967
Maria Bellonci and Niny Garavaglia, *L'opera completa di Mantegna*, Milan, 1967

Berckenhagen 1958
Antoine Pesne: catalogue raisonné, Ekhart Berckenhagen (ed.) in collaboration with Pierre du Colombier, Margarethe Kühn and Georg Poensgen, Berlin, 1958

Berlin 1955
Gemälde der Dresdener Galerie. Übergeben von der Regierung der UdSSR an die Deutsche Demo-kratische Republik, exh. cat., National-Galerie, Berlin, 1955–56

Berlin 1983
Kunst der Reformationszeit, exh. cat., Staatliche Museen (DDR), Berlin, 1983

Berlin 1984
Von Frans Hals bis Vermeer. Meisterwerke holländischer Malerei, exh. cat., Gemäldegalerie Staatliche Museen Preußischer Kulturbesitz, Berlin, 1984

Beutel 1671
Tobias Beutel, *Chur-Fürstlicher Sächsischer stets grünender hoher Cedern-Wald…or Kurtze Vorstellung der Chur-Fürstl. Sächs. Hohen Regal-Werke…*, Dresden, 1671 (reprint Leipzig, 1975)

Bianconi 1781
Gian Lodovico Bianconi, *Historische Lobschrift auf den Ritter Anton Raphael Mengs*, German edition by J. E. W. Müller, Zurich, 1781

Bleyl 1981
Matthias Bleyl, 'Dianas Heimkehr von der Jagd von Rubens. Zur Problematik nachträglicher Formveränderungen', *Kunst in Hessen und am Mittelrhein*, 21, 1981, pp. 53–66

Blunt 1966/67
Anthony Blunt, *Nicolas Poussin*, New York, 1966/67

Boerlin-Brodbeck 1973
Yvonne Boerlin-Brodbeck, 'Antoine Watteau und das Theater', dissertation, Basle, 1973

Bologna 1990
Giuseppe Maria Crespi 1665–1748, Andrea Emiliani and August B. Rave (eds), exh. cat., Pinacoteca Nazionale di Bologna; Staatsgalerie, Stuttgart, 1990–91

Börsch-Supan/Jähnig 1973
Helmut Börsch-Supan with Karl Wilhelm Jähnig, *C. D. Friedrich. Gemälde, Druckgraphik und bildmäßige Zeichnungen*, Munich, 1973

Börsch-Supan 1986
Helmut Börsch-Supan, *Der Maler Antoine Pesne. Franzose und Preuße*, Friedberg, 1986

Boston 1993
Peter C. Sutton, *The Age of Rubens*, exh. cat., Museum of Fine Arts, Boston; Toledo Museum of Fine Arts, 1993–94

Böttger 1972
P. Böttger, *Die alte Pinakothek in München. Architektur, Ausstattung und museales Programm*, Munich, 1972

Brand 1970–71
Erna Brand, 'Untersuchungen zu Albrecht Dürers *Bildnis eines jungen Mannes*', in *Jahrbuch der Staatlichen Kunstsammlungen Dresden*, 1970–71, pp. 59–83

Brown 1986
Jonathan Brown, *Velázquez: Painter and Courtier*, New Haven, 1986

Bürger 2001
Kathrin Bürger, 'Die Gemälde Philips Wouwermans in der Dresdener Gemäldegalerie Alte Meister', 2 vols, dissertation, Dresden, 2001

Camesasca 1974
Ettore Camesasca, *L'opera completa di Bellotto*, Milan, 1974

Camesasca 1992
Ettore Camesasca, *Mantegna*, Milan, 1992

Casanova 1984
Giacomo Casanova, Chevalier de Seingalt, *Geschichte meines Lebens*, Günter Albrecht with Barbara Albrecht (eds), Leipzig and Weimar, 1984

Citati 1996
Pietro Citati, 'Bellotto a Dresda', *Cahiers d'art*, 9, 1996, pp. 40–45

Cocke 1983
Richard Cocke, in London 1983

Cologne 1977
Peter Paul Rubens. 1577–1640, exh. cat., Wallraf-Richartz-Museum, Cologne, 1977

Colombier 1930
Pierre du Colombier, 'Antoine Pesne', in *Les Peintres français du XVIIIe siècle*, Louis Dimier (ed.), 2 vols, Paris and Brussels, 1930

Columbus 1999
Dresden in the Ages of Splendor and Enlightenment. Eighteenth-century Paintings from the Old Master Picture Gallery, Harald Marx and Gregor J. M. Weber (eds), exh. cat., Columbus Museum of Art, Columbus, Ohio, 1999

Constable 1962
W. G. Constable, *Canaletto. Giovanni Antonio Canal 1697–1768*, 2 vols, Oxford, 1962

Constable/Links 1989
W. G. Constable, *Canaletto. Giovanni Antonio Canal 1697–1768*, 2nd edition, revised by J.G. Links, with a supplement, 2 vols, Oxford, 1989

Cremer 1989
Claudia Susannah Cremer, *Hagedorns Geschmack. Studien zur Kunstkennerschaft in Deutschland im 18. Jahrhundert*, Bonn, 1989

Crespi 1769
Luigi Crespi, *Felsina Pittrice. Vite de Pittori Bolognesi. Tomo III che serve di supplemento all'opera del Malvasia*, Rome, 1769

Czok 1989
Karl Czok, *August der Starke und Kursachsen*, Leipzig and Munich, 1989

Da Costa Kaufmann 1989
Thomas Da Costa Kaufmann, *Central European Drawings 1680–1800. A Selection from American Collections*, Princeton, 1989

Delogu 1928
G. Delogu, *Giovanni Benedetto Castiglione detto il grechetto*, Bologna, 1928

Deusch and Winkler 1935
Werner Deusch and Friedrich Winkler, *Deutsche Malerei des 16. Jahrhunderts*, Berlin, 1935

Dijon 2001
Dresde ou le rêve des Princes. La Galerie de peintures au XVIIIe siècle, exh. cat., Musée des Beaux-Arts de Dijon, 2001

Dittrich 1991
Christian Dittrich, 'Gedenkblatt für Carl Heinrich von Heineken', *Dresdener Kunstblätter*, 35, 1991, no. 1, pp.6–14

Dresden Cat. 1812
Beschreibung der kleinen Gemälde- und Kunstsammlung zu Dresden, mit Anmerkungen, 'G.F.W.' (ed.), Dresden, 1812

Dresden Cat. 1817, 1826
Neues Sach- und Ortsverzeichnis der Königlich Sächsischen Gemälde-Gallerie zu Dresden, Dresden, 1817; further edition 1826

Dresden Cat. 1838, 1843
Verzeichnis der königlichen Gemälde-Galerie zu Dresden, Dresden, 1838; further edition 1843

Dresden Cat. 1846, 1848, 1853
Catalog der königlichen Gemälde-Galerie zu Dresden, Dresden, 1846; further editions 1848, 1853

Dresden 1861
Illustrierter Galerie-Führer, Dresden, 1861

Dresden 1899
Deutsche Kunst-Ausstellung, Dresden 1899: Abteilung Cranach-Ausstellung, exh. cat., Blasewitz, Dresden, 1899

Dresden 1968
Venezianische Malerei: 15. bis 18. Jahrhundert, exh. cat., Staatliche Kunstsammlungen (Albertinum), Dresden, 1968

Dresden 1971
Deutsche Kunst der Dürer-Zeit, exh. cat., Staatliche Kunstsammlungen (Albertinum), Dresden, 1971

Dresden 1972
Europäische Landschaftsmalerei 1550–1650, exh. cat., National Galley of Prague; Museum der Bildenden Künste, Budapest; The State Hermitage Museum, Leningrad; Gemäldegalerie Alte Meister Dresden, 1972

Dresden 1976
200 Jahre Malerei in Dresden, exh. cat., Gemäldegalerie Neue Meister, Dresden, 1976

Dresden 1979
Gottfried Semper. Zum 100. Todestag, exh. cat., Staatliche Kunstsammlungen Dresden (Albertinum), Dresden, 1979

Dresden 1987
Gemäldegalerie Dresden Neue Meister – 19. und 20. Jahrhundert, Bestandskatalog und Verzeichnis der beschlagnahmten, vernichteten und vermißten Gemälde, Dresden, 1987

Dresden 1990
Von der Königlichen Kunstakademie zur Hochschule für Bildende Künste (1764–1989), Dresden, 1990

Dresden 1992
Gemäldegalerie Dresden. Alte Meister, Katalog der ausgestellten Werke, Dresden, 1992

Dresden 1998
Zurück in Dresden. Eine Ausstellung ehemals vermisster Werke aus Dresdener Museen, exh. cat., Staatliche Kunstsammlungen Dresden (Schloss), Dresden, 1998

Dresden 2000A
Annegret Laabs, *Von der lustvollen Betrachtung der Bilder. Leidener Feinmaler in der Dresdener Gemäldegalerie*, exh. cat., Gemäldegalerie Alte Meister, Dresden, 2000

Dresden 2000B
Für Sachsen erworben. Schätze des Hauses Wettin, exh. cat., Staatliche Kunstsammlungen Dresden, 2000

Dresden 2000C
Birgit Kloppenburg and Gregor J. M. Weber, *La famosissima Notte! Correggios Gemälde 'Die Heilige Nacht' und seine Wirkungsgeschichte*, exh. cat., Gemäldegalerie Alte Meister, Dresden, 2000

Dresden 2001A
Mengs. Die Erfindung des Klassizismus, Steffi Roettgen (ed.), exh. cat., Staatliche Kunstsammlungen Dresden; Palazzo Zabarella, Padua, 2001

Dresden 2001B
Freunde schenken Kunst 1991–2001, exh. cat., Freunde der Staatlichen Kunstsammlungen Dresden, Kunstsammlungen Dresden, 2001

Düsseldorf 1995
The Lure of Still-life, exh. cat., Galerie Lingenauber, Düsseldorf, 1995

Ebert 1963
Hans Ebert, *Kriegsverluste der Dresdener Gemäldegalerie. Vernichtete und vermisste Werke*, Dresden, 1963

Eckardt 1957
Götz Eckardt, *Antoine Pesne. Katalog der Gedächtnisausstellung zum 200. Todestag*, Potsdam-Sanssouci, 1957

Eckardt 1974
Götz Eckardt, 'Die Bildergalerie in Sanssouci. Zur Geschichte des Bauwerkes und seiner Sammlungen bis zur Mitte des 19. Jahrhunderts', dissertation, Halle, 1974

Ehrenstein 1923
Thomas Ehrenstein, *Das Alte Testament im Bild*, Vienna, 1923

Essen 1986
Barock in Dresden 1694–1763. Kunst und Kunstsammlungen unter der Regierung des Kurfürsten Friedrich August I. von Sachsen und Königs August II. von Polen, exh. cat., Villa Hügel, Essen, 1986

Evers 1942
Hans G. Evers, *Peter Paul Rubens*, Munich, 1942

Félibien 1685–88
André Félibien, *Entretiens sur la vie et les ouvrages des plus excellents peintres anciens et modernes*, 5 vols, Paris 1666–88; 8ème entretien, 4, 'Nicolas Poussin', Paris, 1685

Femmel 1980
Gerhard Femmel, *Die Franzosen. Goethes Graphiksammlung*, Munich, 1980

Ferrara 2002
Il Trionfo di Bacco. Capolavori della scuola ferrarese a Dresda 1480–1620, exh. cat., Gregor J. M. Weber (ed.), Castello Estense, Ferrara, 2002

Ferré 1972
Jean Ferré et al., *Watteau*, 4 vols, Madrid and Paris, 1972

Feuchtmayr 1921
Karl Feuchtmayr, 'Die Malerfamilie Apt', in *Münchner Jahrbuch für bildende Kunst*, 11, 1921, pp.54–57

Feuchtmayr 1928
Karl Feuchtmayr, 'Apt-Studien', in *Augsburger Kunst der Spätgotik und Renaissance*, Ernst Buchner and Karl Feuchtmayr (eds), Augsburg, 1928

Fiorillo 1805
Johann Dominicus Fiorillo, *Geschichte der Malerei*, vol. 3, Göttingen, 1805

Florence 1982
Dresda sull'Arno. Da Cranach a Van Gogh e oltre. 100 Capolavori dalla Pinacoteca di Dresda, exh. cat., Palazzo Pitti, Florence, 1982–83

Fort Worth 1986
Giuseppe Maria Crespi and the Emergence of Genre Painting in Italy, exh. cat., Kimbell Art Museum, Fort Worth, 1986

Frankfurt 1966
Adam Elsheimer. Werk, künstlerische Herkunft und Nachfolge, exh. cat., Städelsches Kunstinstitut, Frankfurt am Main, 1966

Frankfurt 1994
Goethe und die Kunst, Sabine Schulze (ed.), exh. cat., Schirn Kunsthalle, Frankfurt am Main; Kunstsammlungen zu Weimar, 1994

Friedländer 1914
Walter Friedländer, *Nicolas Poussin. Die Entwicklung seiner Kunst*, Munich, 1914

Friedländer 1965
Walter Friedländer, *Nicolas Poussin*, Paris, 1965

Friedländer and Rosenberg 1932
Max J. Friedländer and Jakob Rosenberg, *Die Gemälde von Lukas Cranach*, Berlin, 1932

Friedländer and Rosenberg 1989
Max J. Friedländer and Jakob Rosenberg, *Die Gemälde von Lukas Cranach*, 2nd edition, Stuttgart, 1989

Fritzsche 1936
Hellmuth Allwill Fritzsche, *Bernardo Bellotto genannt Canaletto*, Burg bei Magdeburg, 1936

Fudickar 1942
Lieselotte Fudickar, 'Die Bildniskunst der Nürnberger Barthel Beham und Peter Gertner', dissertation, Munich, 1942

Gaehtgens 1992
Thomas W. Gaehtgens, *Die Berliner Museumsinsel im Deutschen Kaiserreich*, Munich, 1992

Garrido Pérez 1992
Carmen Garrido Pérez, *Velázquez. Técnica y evolución*, exh. cat., Museo del Prado, Madrid, 1992

Gemar-Koeltzsch 1995
Erika Gemar-Koeltzsch, *Holländische Stillebenmaler im 17. Jahrhundert*, 3 vols, Lingen, 1995

Gemin and Pedrocco 1993
M. Gemin and F. Pedrocco, *Giambattista Tiepolo. I dipinti. Opera completa*, Venice, 1993

Genoa 1990
Il genio di Giovanni Benedetto Castiglione. Il Grechetto, G. Dillon (ed.), exh. cat., Ministero per i Beni Culturali e Ambientali, Genoa, 1990

Gessner 1787/88 (1801)
Salomon Gessners Briefwechsel mit seinem Sohne. Während dem Aufenthalte der letzteren in Dresden und Rom in den Jahren 1784/85 und 1787/88, Bern/Zürich, 1801

Göpfert 1972
Hans Jörg Göpfert, *Johann Alexander Thiele. Leben und Werk*, Leipzig, 1914

Grautoff 1914
Otto Grautoff, *Nicolas Poussin. Sein Werk und sein Leben*, 2 vols, Munich and Leipzig, 1914

Greindl 1956
Edith Greindl, *Les Peintres flamands de nature morte au XVIIe siècle*, Brussels, 1956

Guinard 1967
Paul Guinard, *Dauzats et Blanchard. Peintres de l'Espagne romantique*, Paris, 1967

Haake 1927
Paul Haake, *August der Starke*, Berlin and Leipzig, 1927

Hagedorn 1762
Christian Ludwig von Hagedorn, *Betrachtungen über die Mahlerey*, Leipzig, 1762

Hagedorn/Baden 1797
Christian Ludwig von Hagedorn, *Lettre à un amateur de la peinture avec des éclaircissements historiques sur un cabinet…Dresde 1755. Briefe über die Kunst von Christian Ludwig von Hagedorn*, Torkel Baden (ed.), Leipzig, 1797

Hamburg 2002
Meisterwerke aus Dresden zu Gast im Bucerius Kunst Forum Hamburg, exh. cat., Bucerius Kunst Forum, Hamburg, 2002

Hantzsch 1902
Viktor Hantzsch, 'Beiträge zur älteren Geschichte der kurfürstlichen Kunstkammer in Dresden', in *Neues Archiv für sächsische Geschichte und Altertumskunde*, 23, 1902, pp.220–96

Hasche 1781–83
Johann Christian Hasche, *Umständliche Beschreibung Dresdens, mit seinen äußeren und innern Merkwürdigkeiten. Historisch und architektonisch mit zugegebenem Grundriss*, 2 vols, Leipzig, 1781–83

Heidelberg 1964
Kunst in Dresden, exh. cat., Kurpfälzisches Museum, Heidelberg, 1964

Heineken 1753–57
Recueil d'estampes d'après les plus célèbres tableaux de la Galerie Royale de Dresde, Carl Heinrich von Heineken (ed.), 2 vols, Dresden, 1753–57

Hentschel 1973
Walter Hentschel, *Denkmale sächsischer Kunst. Die Verluste des zweiten Weltkriegs*, Berlin, 1973

Heres 1982
Gerald Heres, 'Die Dresdener Kunstsammlungen in Keyßlers "Neuesten Reisen"', in *Jahrbuch der Staatlichen Kunstsammlungen Dresden*, 11, 1978–79 (1982), p.105

Heres 1983
Gerald Heres, 'Der Zwinger als Museum', in *Jahrbuch der Staatlichen Kunstsammlungen Dresden*, 12, 1980 (1983), pp.119–33

Heres 1991A
Gerald Heres, *Dresdener Kunstsammlungen im 18. Jahrhundert*, Leipzig, 1991

Heres 1991B
Gerald Heres, *Winckelmann in Sachsen. Ein Beitrag zur Kulturgeschichte Dresdens und zur Biographie Winckelmanns*, Berlin and Leipzig, 1991

Hildebrandt 1922
Edmundt Hildebrandt, *Antoine Watteau*, Berlin, 1922

Hirt 1830
A. Hirt, *Kunstbemerkungen auf einer Reise über Wittenberg und Meissen nach Dresden und Prag*, Berlin, 1830

Hoffmann 1992
Helga Hoffmann, *Die deutschen Gemälde des XVI. Jahrhunderts*, Weimar, 1992

Holzhausen 1927
Walter Holzhausen, 'Lage und Rekonstruktion der kurfürstlichen Kunstkammer im Schloß zu Dresden', *Repertorium für Kunstwissenschaft*, 48, 1927, pp.140–47

Holzhausen 1940
Walter Holzhausen, 'Antoine Pesne und seine Beziehungen zu August dem Starken', *Zeitschrift für Kunstgeschichte*, 9, 1940, pp.49–65

Honisch 1960
Dieter Honisch, 'Anton Raphael Mengs und die Bildform des Frühklassizismus', dissertation, Münster, 1960

Hübner 1856
Julius Hübner, *Verzeichnis der Königlichen Gemälde-Gallerie zu Dresden. Mit einer historischen Einleitung*, Dresden, 1856

Hübner 1868
Julius Hübner, *Verzeichnis der Königlichen Gemälde-Gallerie zu Dresden. Mit einer historischen Einleitung*, Dresden, 1868

Hübner 1872
Julius Hübner, *Verzeichnis der Königlichen Gemälde-Gallerie zu Dresden. Mit einer historischen Einleitung*, Dresden, 1872

Hübner 1884
Julius Hübner, *Verzeichnis der Königlichen Gemälde-Gallerie zu Dresden. Mit einer historischen Einleitung*, Dresden, 1884

Hulst 1966
R.-A. d'Hulst, 'Enkele onbekende schilderijen van Jakob Jordaens', *Gentse Bijdragen tot de Kunstgeschiedenis en de Oudheidkunde*, 19, 1961–66, pp. 81–94

Hulst 1982
R.-A. d'Hulst, *Jacob Jordaens*, Stuttgart, 1982

Inv. Dresden 1722–28
Lit. A. et B. Inventaria Sr. Königl. Majestät in Pohlen und Churfürstl. Durchl. zu Sachsen große, wie auch kleine Cabinets und andere Schildereyen. Extract Derjenigen Königlichen Schildereyen, welche Mense Julii 1722 bey gehaltener Comißarischen Inventirung sich in Vorrath befunden. Item, was nach dem darzu erkaufft und geliefert, oder von andern Königl. Schlössern zur Einnahme zu bringen angegeben, und wo dato dieselbe aufgemacht sind, ist zu ersehen, wie folget: Ex Libro Inventarii sub Lit: A. Extrahirt Mense Aug. ao 1728, compiled by Johann Adam Steinhäuser, 1722–28

Inv. Dresden 1754
Inventarium von der Königlichen Bilder-Galerie zu Dreßden, gefertiget Mens: Julij & August: 1754, compiled by Matthias Oesterreich, 1754

Inv. Guarienti 1747–50
Catalogo delli quadri, che sono nel Gabinetto di Sua Maestà, compiled by Pietro Guarienti, 1747–50

Inv. 'vor 1741' in 8°
Sr. königl. Maj. in Polen und kurfürstl. Durchl. zu Sachsen Schilderei-Inventaria sub Lit. A et. B., compiled by Johann Adam Steinhäuser

Jaffé 1977
Michael Jaffé, *Rubens and Italy*, Oxford, 1977

Jongh 1968–69
Eddie de Jongh, 'Erotica in vogelperspectief. De dubbelzinnigheid van een 17de-eeuwse genrevorst', *Simiolus*, 3, 1968–69, pp. 22–74

Justi 1903
Carl Justi, *Diego Velázquez und sein Jahrhundert*, 2 vols, 2nd edition, Bonn, 1903

Kauffmann 1963
H. Kauffmann, 'Zweckbau und Monument. Schinkels Museum am Berliner Lustgarten', in *Eine Festgabe für Ernst Hellmut Vits*, Frankfurt am Main, 1963

Keyssler 1751
Johann George Keyssler, *Neueste Reisen durch Teutschland, Böhmen, Ungarn, die Schweiz, Italien und Lothringen*, Hanover, 1741; 2nd edition, 1751

Kitson 1978
Michael Kitson, *Claude Lorrain. Liber Veritatis*, London, 1978

Knab 1967–68
Eckhard Knab, 'Über Bernini, Poussin und Le Brun', *Albertina Studien*, 5–6, 1967–68, pp. 3–32

Knapp 1968
Norbert Knapp, 'Watteaus neue Bildform', in *Festschrift für Werner Gross*, Munich, 1968

Knox 1992
George Knox, *Giambattista Piazzetta 1682–1754*, Oxford, 1992

Kolb 2002
Karin Kolb, 'Die Rezeption Dürers durch Lucas Cranach den Jüngeren am Beispiel des erwachten Herkules', *Dresdener Kunstblätter*, 46, 2002, no. 4, pp. 118–26

Kozakiewicz 1972
Stefan Kozakiewicz, *Bernardo Bellotto genannt Canaletto*, 2 vols, Recklinghausen, 1972

Kramer 1916
Oskar Kramer, *Der Bau der Modernen Gemäldegalerie in Dresden*, in *Mitteilungen aus den Sächsischen Kunstsammlungen*, commissioned by the Generaldirektion of the Königlichen Sammlungen zu Dresden, 7, 1916, pp. 112–19

Kurth 1956
Willy Kurth, 'Zu den Dresdener Bildern von Watteau', *Bildende Kunst*, 5, 1956, pp. 253–55

Larsen 1952
Erik Larsen, *Peter Paul Rubens. With a Complete Catalogue of His Works in America*, Antwerp, 1952

Larsen 1988
Erik Larsen, *The Paintings of Anthony van Dyck*, 2 vols, Freren, 1988

LCI 1968–76
Lexikon der christlichen Ikonographie, founded by Engelbert Kirschbaum, Wolfgang Braunfels (ed.), 8 vols, Rome, Freiburg, Basle and Vienna, 1968–76

Legenda Aurea 1979
Jacobus de Voragine, *Legenda Aurea*, Richard Benz (ed.), Heidelberg, 1979

Lehninger 1782
Johann August Lehninger, *Abrégé de la vie des peintres dont les tableaux composent la Galerie Electorale de Dresde*, Dresden, 1782

Leiden 2001
The Leiden Fijnschilders from Dresden, Annegret Laabs (ed.), with a contribution by Christoph Schölzel, exh. cat., Stedelijk Museum de Lakenhal, Leiden, 2001

Levey 1988
Michael Levey, *Giambattista Tiepolo. La sua vita, la sua arte*, Milan, 1988

Liebmann 1972
Michael Liebmann, *Deutsche Malerei in den Museen der Sowjetunion*, Leningrad, 1972

Lindau 1856
Martin Bernhard Lindau, *Dresdener Galeriebuch. Ein berathender Führer zur Auffindung und zum Verständnis sämtlicher Meisterwerke in der Königl. Gemälde-Gallerie*, Dresden, 1856

Lindau 1883
Martin Bernhard Lindau, *Lucas Cranach. Ein Lebensbild aus dem Zeitalter der Reformation*, Leipzig, 1883

Lindau 1885
Martin Bernhard Lindau, *Geschichte der königlichen Haupt- und Residenzstadt Dresden von den ältesten Zeiten bis zur Gegenwart*, 2nd edition, Dresden, 1885

Lippold 1963
G. Lippold, *Bernardo Bellotto genannt Canaletto*, Leipzig, 1963

Löcher 1999
Kurt Löcher, *Barthel Beham. Ein Maler aus dem Dürerkreis*, Munich and Berlin, 1999

Löffler 1985
Fritz Löffler, *Bernardo Bellotto, genannt Canaletto. Dresden im 18. Jahrhundert*, Leipzig, 1985

Löffler 2000
Fritz Löffler, *Bernardo Bellotto, genannt Canaletto. Dresden im 18. Jahrhundert*, Munich and Berlin, 2000

London 1983
The Genius of Venice 1500–1600, exh. cat., Royal Academy of Arts, London, 1983

London 1994
The Glory of Venice: Art in the Eighteenth Century, Jane Martineau and Andrew Robison (eds), exh. cat., Royal Academy of Arts, London; National Gallery of Art, Washington DC, 1994

London 2001
Xanthe Brooke and Peter Cherry, *Murillo: Scenes of Childhood*, exh. cat., Dulwich Picture Gallery, London, 2001

López-Rey 1996A
José López-Rey, *Velázquez: catalogue raisonné*, Cologne, 1996

López-Rey 1996B
José López-Rey, *Velázquez: Painter of Painters*, Cologne, 1996

Madrid 1992
Ribera. 1591–1652, Alfonso E. Pérez Sanchez and Nicola Spinosa (eds), exh. cat., Museo del Prado, Madrid, 1992

Madrid 1998
Obras maestras del siglo XVIII en la Galería de Pinturas de Dresde. Creación y Coleccionismo Regio en Sajonia, Harald Marx and Juan J. Luna (eds), exh. cat., Banco Bilbao Vizcaya, Madrid, 1998

Madrid 1999
Velázquez, Rubens y van Dyck. Pintures cortesanos del siglo XVII, exh. cat., Museo Nacional del Prado, Madrid, 1999

Magne 1914
Emile Magne, *Nicolas Poussin. Premier peintre du roi. 1594–1665*, Brussels and Paris, 1914

Malvasia 1678
Carlo Cesare Malvasia, *Felsina Pittrice. Vite de' pittori Bolognesi*, Bologna, 1678

Mariusz 1982
Adriano Mariusz, *L'opera completa del Piazzetta*, Milan, 1982

Marx 1973
Harald Marx, 'Französische Malerei des 18. Jahrhunderts in der Dresdener Gemäldegalerie. Die ausgestellten Bilder', *Dresdener Kunstblätter*, 17, 1973, no. 6, pp. 174–88

Marx 1974
Harald Marx, *Neuerwerbungen Deutscher Malerei*, Staatliche Kunstsammlungen, Dresden, 1974

Marx 1982
Harald Marx, 'Das Entstehen der Sammlung spanischer Gemälde in der Dresdener Galerie. Ludwig Gruner zum 100. Todestag', *Dresdener Kunstblätter*, 26, 1982, pp. 42–55

Marx 1985
'Barocke Bildnismalerei in Dresden von der Mitte des 17. Jahrhunderts bis zum Ende der "augusteischen" Zeit', in *Jahrbuch der Staatlichen Kunstsammlungen Dresden 1985*, Dresden, 1987, pp. 51–84

Marx 1990
Harald Marx, 'Malerei im Königlichen Dresden', in Munich 1990, pp. 23–28

Marx 1993
Harald Marx, 'Wiedereröffnung der Dresdener Gemäldegalerie Alte Meister im Semperbau am Zwinger', *Sächsische Heimatblätter*, 39, 1993, no. 2, pp. 65–71

Marx 1994A
Harald Marx, 'Pan und Syrinx. Eine Metamorphose nach Ovid. Kabinettausstellung in der Gemäldegalerie Alte Meister', *Dresdener Kunstblätter*, 38, 1994, no. 6, pp. 163–68

Marx 1994B
Harald Marx, 'Christus am Kreuz aus Wolken gebildet. Eine Neuerwerbung der Gemäldegalerie Alte Meister', *Dresdener Kunstblätter*, 38, 1994, no. 5, pp. 134–38

Marx 1999A
Harald Marx, 'Das Bildnis des Charles de Solier, Sieur de Morette, von Hans Holbein dem Jüngeren', in *Hans Holbein der Jüngere. Akten des Internationalen Symposiums Kunstmuseum Basel, 26.–28. Juni 1997*, Basle, 1999, pp. 263–79

Marx 1999B
Harald Marx, 'The Dresden Gemäldegalerie as "Ecole publique" in the Eighteenth Century', in Columbus 1999, pp. 30–39

Marx 2000A
Harald Marx, 'Das Entstehen der Sammlung spanischer Gemälde in der Dresdener Galerie', in *Dresden und Spanien. Akten des interdisziplinären Kolloquiums Dresden 1998*, Christoph Rodieck (ed.), Frankfurt am Main, 2000, pp. 67–84

Marx 2000B
Harald Marx, 'Von Louis de Silvestre zu Anton Graff. Die Bildnisse des Johann George Chevalier de Saxe', in *Jahrbuch der Staatlichen Kunstsammlungen Dresden*, 28, 2000, pp. 57–66

Marx 2001
Harald Marx, 'Carl Heinrich von Heineken et Pierre Jean Mariette, ou "du plaisir de former des Amateurs et des Artistes"', in Dijon 2001, pp. 149–57

Marx 2002A
Harald Marx, *Die schönsten Ansichten aus Sachsen. Johann Alexander Thiele (1685–1752). Zum 250. Todestag*, exh. cat., Gemäldegalerie Alte Meister, Dresden, 2002

Marx 2002B
Harald Marx, *Gemäldegalerie Dresden. Alte Meister. Führer*, 2nd edition, Leipzig, 2002

Matthäi 1834
Friedrich Matthäi, *Beschreibung der neu errichteten Sammlung vaterländischer Prospekte von Alexander Thiele und Canaletto*, Dresden, 1834

Matthäi 1835, 1837
Friedrich Matthäi, *Verzeichnis der Königlich-Sächsischen Gemälde-Galerie zu Dresden*, Dresden, 1835, 1837

Mayer 1923
A. L. Mayer, *Jusepe di Ribera (Lo Spagnoletto)*, Leipzig, 1923

McFadyen Felton 1971
Craig McFadyen Felton, 'Jusepe di Ribera. A Catalogue Raisonné', dissertation, Pittsburgh, 1971

Menz 1962
Henner Menz, *Die Dresdener Gemäldegalerie*, Munich and Zurich, 1962

Menz 1984
Henner Menz, 'Die Dresdener Gemäldegalerie im Semperbau 1855–1960', in *Jahrbuch der Staatlichen Kunstsammlungen Dresden*, 16, 1984, pp. 81–110

Menzhausen 1985
Joachim Menzhausen, 'Kurfürst Augusts Kunstkammer. Eine Analyse des Inventars von 1587', in *Jahrbuch der Staatlichen Kunstsammlungen Dresden*, 17, 1985, pp. 21–29

Merriman 1980
Mira Pajes Merriman, *Giuseppe Maria Crespi*, Milan, 1980

Mexico 1980
50 Obras maestas de Pintura de los Museos de Dresden y Berlin, Harald Marx (ed.), exh. cat., Museo San Carlo, Mexico City, 1980

Michel 1984
Petra Michel, *Christian Wilhelm Ernst Dietrich (1712–1774) und die Problematik des Eklektizismus*, Munich, 1984

Michel 1999
Patrick Michel, *Mazarin, prince des collectionneurs. Les collections et l'ameublement du Cardinal Mazarin (1602–1661). Histoire et analyse*, Paris, 1999

Michel 2001
Patrick Michel, '"Peintre et négociant en tableaux, et autres curiosités. Bon connoisseur." Esquisse d'un portrait', in *Mélanges en hommage à Pierre Rosenberg. Peintures et dessins en France et en Italie XVIIe–XVIIIe siècle*, Paris, 2001, pp. 328–36

Monschau-Schmittmann 1993
Birgid Monschau-Schmittmann, *Julius Hübner (1806–1882). Leben und Werk eines Malers der Spätromantik* (Bonner Studien zur Kunstgeschichte, vol. 7), Münster and Hamburg, 1993

Moscow 1995
Pushkin State Museum of Fine Arts. Catalogue of Painting, I. E. Danilova (ed.), Moscow, 1995

Munich 1983
Im Licht von Claude Lorrain, exh. cat., Haus der Kunst, Munich, 1983

Munich 1990
Königliches Dresden. Kunst im 18. Jahrhundert, exh. cat., Kunsthalle der Hypo-Kulturstiftung, Munich, 1990

Munich 1998
Die Nacht, exh. cat., Haus der Kunst, Munich, 1998

Munich 2000
Venus. Bilder einer Göttin, exh. cat., Alte Pinakothek, Munich, 2000–01

Münster 1979
Stilleben in Europa, exh. cat., Westfälisches Landesmuseum, Münster, 1979

Murcia 2002
Huellas. Catedral de Murcia, exh. cat., Murcia Cathedral, 2002

Nemilowa 1964
Inna Sergejewna Nemilowa, *Watteau und seine Werke in der Eremitage*, Leningrad, 1964

New York 1985
The Age of Caravaggio, exh. cat., Metropolitan Museum of Art, New York, 1985

New York 1992
Jusepe di Ribera. 1591–1652, Alfonso E. Pérez Sanchez and Nicola Spinosa (eds), exh. cat., Metropolitan Museum of Art, New York, 1992

Noble 1972
M. Noble, 'Abraham Mignon 1640–1679. Beiträge zur Stilleben-malerei im 17. Jahrhundert', dissertation, Stuttgart, 1972

Oelsner and Prinz 1985
Norbert Oelsner and Henning Prinz, 'Zur politisch-kulturellen Funktion des Dresdner Residenzschlosses vom 16. bis 18. Jahrhundert', *Sächsische Heimatblätter*, 31, 1985, p.247

Osten 1973
Gert von der Osten, 'Noch ein Bildnis eines Mannes vor freiem Himmel von Wolf Huber', in *Wallraf-Richartz-Jahrbuch*, 35, 1973, pp.207–26

Panofsky 1948
Erwin Panofsky, *Albrecht Dürer*, vol. 1, Princeton, 1948

Paris 1977
Pèlerinage à Watteau, exh. cat., Hôtel de la Monnaie, Paris, 1977

Paris 1984
Diderot et l'art de Boucher à David. Les Salons. 1759–1781, exh. cat., Hôtel de la Monnaie, Paris, 1984

Paris 1987
Subleyras 1699–1749, exh. cat., Musée du Luxembourg, Paris; Villa Medici, Rome, 1987

Paris 1990
Jacques Thuillier et al., *Vouet*, exh. cat., Galeries Nationales du Grand Palais, Paris, 1990

Paris 1993
Le Siècle de Titien. L'âge d'or de la peinture à Venise, exh. cat., Grand Palais, Paris, 1993

Parthey 1861–64
Gustav Parthey, *Deutscher Bildersaal*, 2 vols, Berlin, 1861–64

Pedrocco 2000
Filippo Pedrocco, *Tiziano*, Milan, 2000

Pérez Sánchez and Spinosa 1978
Alfonso E. Pérez Sánchez and Nicola Spinosa, *L'opera completa del Ribera*, Milan, 1978

Petropoulos 1999
Jonathan Petropoulos, *Kunstraub und Sammelwahn. Kunst und Politik im Dritten Reich*, Berlin, 1999

Phillips 1895
Claude Phillips, *Antoine Watteau*, London, 1895

Pichon 1880
Jérôme Baron de Pichon, *La Vie de Charles-Henry Comte de Hoym, Ambassadeur de Saxe-Pologne en France et célèbre amateur de livres, 1694–1736*, 2 vols, Paris, 1880

Pignatti 1976
Teresio Pignatti, *Veronese*, 2 vols, Venice, 1976

Pilon 1924
Edmond Pilon, *Watteau et son école*, 2nd edition, Paris and Brussels, 1924

Plagemann 1967
Volker Plagemann, *Das deutsche Kunstmuseum 1790–1870*, Munich, 1967

Polazzo 1990
Marco Polazzo, *Pietro Rotari. Pittore veronese del Settecento*, Verona, 1990

Posner 1971
Donald Posner, *Annibale Carracci. A Study in the Reform of Italian Painting Around 1590*, 2 vols, London, 1971

Posse 1911
Hans Posse, 'Die Umgestaltung der Dresdner Gemäldegalerie', in *Mitteilungen aus den Sächsischen Kunstsammlungen*, Dresden, 1911, pp.60–70

Posse 1920
Hans Posse, *Katalog der Staatlichen Gemäldegalerie zu Dresden. 1. Teil: Alte Meister*, Dresden and Berlin, 1920

Posse 1929
Hans Posse, *Die Staatliche Gemälde-galerie zu Dresden. Vollständiges beschreibendes Verzeichnis der älteren Gemälde. I. Abteilung: Die romanischen Länder*, Dresden and Berlin, 1929

Posse 1930
Hans Posse, *Die Staatliche Gemäldegalerie zu Dresden. Katalog der Alten Meister*, Dresden and Berlin, 1930

Posse 1931
Hans Posse, 'Die Briefe des Grafen Francesco Algarotti an dem sächsischen Hof und seine Bilderkäufe für die Dresdner Gemäldegalerie 1743–47', in *Jahrbuch der Preussischen Kunstsammlungen Berlin*, 52, 1931, pp.1–73

Posse 1932
Hans Posse, 'Zwei Bildnisse sächsischer Kurfürsten von Lucas Cranach d. Ä.', *Pantheon*, 1932, pp.73–74

Posse 1937A
Hans Posse, 'Lahmanns Vermächtnis', *Dresdner Nachrichten*, 23 December 1937

Posse 1937B
Hans Posse, *Die Gemäldegalerie zu Dresden. Die alten Meister*, Dresden, undated [1937]

Posse 1942
Hans Posse, *Lucas Cranach der Altere*, Vienna, 1942

Potsdam 1983
Gerd Bartoscheck, *Antoine Pesne 1683–1757*, exh. cat., Schloss Sanssouci, Potsdam, 1983

Prause 1954
Marianne Prause, *Das Elbsandstein-gebirge und die Dresdener Landschaft in der deutschen Malerei*, Leipzig, 1954

Quandt 1842
J. G. von Quandt, *Über den Zustand der Königlichen Gemäldegalerie zu Dresden. Für wahre Freunde der Kunst, nebst Belegen und erläuternden Anmerkungen*, Leipzig, 1842

Quandt 1856
J. G. von Quandt, *Der Begleiter durch die Gemälde-Säle des Königlichen Museums zu Dresden*, Dresden, 1856

Raumschüssel 1987
M. Raumschüssel, in *Matthäus Daniel Pöppelmann 1662–1736. Ein Architekt des Barocks in Dresden*, exh. cat., Staatliche Kunstsammlungen Dresden, 1987

Renckens and Duyvetter 1959
B.J.A. Renckens and J. Duyvetter, 'De Vrouw van Gabriel Metsu, Isabella de Wolff, geboortig van Enkhuizen', *Oud Holland*, 74, 1959, pp.179–82

Rethel 1912
Alfred Rethel, *Alfred Rethels Briefe*, Josef Ponten (ed.), Berlin, 1912

Reyher 1961
U. Reyher, *Johann Alexander Thiele. Ein Dresdner Landschaftsmaler des Spätbarock*, Leipzig, 1961

Riedel and Wenzel 1765
Johann Anton Riedel and Christian Friedrich Wenzel, *Catalogue des tableaux de la Galerie électorale à Dresde*, Dresden, 1765

Riedel 1801
Johann Anton Riedel, *Verzeichniss der Gemälde, welche in der Churfürstl. Gallerie zu Dresden befindlich sind*, Dresden, 1801

Riedel 1806
Johann Anton Riedel, *Beschreibung der churfürstlichen Gemaelde-Galerie in Dresden mit Anmerkungen und einem alphabetischen Künstler-Verzeichnisse*, Dresden, 1806

Riemann 1966
G. Riemann, 'Schinkels Altes Museum. Zu seiner Bedeutung und Geschichte', in *Das Alte Museum 1823–1866. Festschrift zur Wiedereröffnung*, 1966, Berlin, 1966, pp.7–30

Rizzi 1996
Alberto Rizzi, *Bernardo Bellotto. Dresda – Vienna – Monaco 1747–1766*, Venice, 1996

Robels 1989
Hella Robels, *Frans Snyders. Stilleben- und Tiermaler 1579–1657*, Munich, 1989

Robinson 1974
Franklin W. Robinson, *Gabriel Metsu (1629–1667). A Study of His Place in Dutch Genre Painting of the Golden Age*, New York, 1974

Roethlisberger 1968
Claude Lorrain. The Drawings, Marcel Roethlisberger (ed.), Berkeley, 1968

Roethlisberger 1979
Marcel Roethlisberger, *Claude Lorrain. The Paintings*, 2 vols, New York, 1979 (1st edition 1961)

Roethlisberger 1986
Marcel Roethlisberger, *Tout l'oeuvre peint de Claude Lorrain*, Paris, 1986

Roettgen 1993
Steffi Roettgen, 'Introduction', in *Anton Raphael Mengs (1728–1779) and His British Patrons*, exh. cat., Kenwood House (The Iveagh Bequest), London, 1993, pp.9–42

Roettgen 1999
Steffi Roettgen, *Anton Raphael Mengs 1728–1779. Bd. I: Das malerische und zeichnerische Werk*, Munich, 1999

Rome 1959
Il Settecento a Roma, exh. cat., Palazzo delle Esposizioni, Rome, 1959

Rome 2001
Velázquez, exh. cat., Fondazione Memmo, Rome, 2001

Rosenberg 1896
Adolf Rosenberg, *Antoine Watteau*, Bielefeld and Leipzig, 1896

Rosenberg 1987
Pierre Rosenberg, 'Répétitions et répliques dans l'oeuvre de Watteau', in *Antoine Watteau (1684–1721). Le peintre, son temps et sa légende*, Paris and Geneva, 1987, pp.103–10

Rosenthal 1929
Shelly Rosenthal, 'Russische Kunsthistorische Literatur', *Repertorium für Kunstwissenschaft*, 50, 1929, pp.39–41

Runge 1981
Philipp Otto Runge, *Briefe und Schriften*, Peter Betthausen (ed.), Berlin, 1981

Sacher 1981
Gerthilde Sacher, 'Die Abnahme einer Übermalung auf einem Bild von Teniers d. J.', in *Jahrbuch der Staatlichen Kunstsammlungen Dresden*, 13, 1981, pp.37–41

Salmon 1997
Xavier Salmon, in *Louis de Silvestre. Un peintre français à la cour de Dresde*, exh. cat., Musée National du Château de Versailles, 1997

Sandrart 1675–80 (1994)
Joachim von Sandrart, *Teutsche Academie der Bau-, Bild- und Mahlerey-Künste*, vols 1–3, Nuremberg 1675–80; new edition with an introduction by Christian Klemm, Nördlingen, 1994

Schaar 1958
Eckhard Schaar, *Studien zu Nicolaes Berchem*, Cologne, 1958

Schäfer 1860
Wilhelm Schäfer, *Die Königliche Gemälde-Gallerie im Neuen Museum zu Dresden*, 3 vols, Dresden, 1860

Schilling 1843–44
Anton Raphael Mengs sämtliche hinterlassene Schriften. Gesammelt, nach den Originaltexten neu übersetzt und mit mehreren Beilagen und Anmerkungen vermehrt, G. Schilling (ed.), Bonn, 1843–44

Schlechte 1992
Horst Schlechte, *Das geheime politische Tagebuch des Kurprinzen Friedrich Christian 1751–57*, Weimar, 1992

Schmidt 1917
H. Schmidt, 'Gottorfer Künstler', in *Quellen und Forschungen zur Geschichte Schleswig-Holsteins*, 5, 1917, pp.335–56

Schmidt 2000
Bernardo Bellotto genannt Canaletto in Pirna und auf der Festung Königstein, Werner Schmidt (ed.), Pirna, 2000

Schoen 2001
Christian Schoen, *Albrecht Dürer. Adam und Eva. Die Gemälde, ihre Geschichte und Rezeption bei Lucas Cranach d. Ä. und Hans Baldung Grien*, Berlin, 2001

Schramm 1744
Carl Christian Schramm, *Neues Europäisches Historisches Reise-Lexicon…*, Leipzig, 1744

Schuchardt 1851
Christian Schuchardt, *Lucas Cranach des Älteren Leben und Werke*, vol. 2, Leipzig, 1851

Schulz 1846
H. W. Schulz, *Über die Nothwendig-keit eines neuen Galleriegebäudes für die Königl. Gemäldesammlung*, Leipzig, 1846

Schumacher 1989
Birgit Schumacher, *Studien zu Werk und Wirkung Philips Wouwermans*, Munich, 1989

Seelig 1977
L. Seelig, in *Barockplastik in Norddeutschland*, exh. cat., Museum für Kunst und Gewerbe Hamburg, Mainz, 1977

Segal 1988
Sam Segal, *A Prosperous Past. The Sumptous Still-life in the Netherlands 1600–1700*, The Hague, 1988

Seling 1952
H. Seling, 'Die Entstehung des Kunstmuseums', dissertation, Freiburg im Breisgau, 1952

Seydewitz 1957
Ruth and Max Seydewitz, *Das Dresdner Galeriebuch. Vierhundert Jahre Dresdner Gemäldegalerie*, Dresden, 1957

Slive 2001
Seymour Slive, *Jacob van Ruisdael. A Complete Catalogue of His Paintings, Drawings and Etchings*, New Haven and London, 2001

Sponsel 1906
Jean-Louis Sponsel, *Fürstenbildnisse aus dem Haus Wettin*, Dresden, 1906

Staszewski 1996
Jacek Staszewski, *August der III. Kurfürst von Sachsen and König von Polen*, Berlin, 1996

Stephan 2001
B. Stephan, in *Hauptsache Köpfe, Plastische Porträts von der Renaissance bis zur Gegenwart aus der Skulpturensammlung*, exh. cat., Staatliche Kunstsammlungen Dresden, Skulpturensammlung, 2001

Stübel 1912
Moritz Stübel, *Christian Ludwig von Hagedorn. Ein Diplomat und Sammler des 18. Jahrhunderts*, Leipzig, 1912

Stübel 1914
Moritz Stübel, *Der Landschaftsmaler Johann Alexander Thiele und seine sächsischen Prospekte*, Berlin, 1914

Stübel 1923
Moritz Stübel, *Canaletto*, Berlin and Dresden, 1923

Stübel 1924–25
Moritz Stübel, 'Dresdner Sammler des 18. Jahrhunderts', in *Das Sammlerkabinett. Bücher – Kunst – Antiquitäten*, 3/10, 1924–25, pp.1–6

Thieme/Becker 1907–50
Thieme/Becker, *Allgemeines Künstler-Lexikon*, 37 vols, Leipzig, 1907–50

Thuillier 1974
Jacques Thuillier, *L'opera completa di Poussin*, Milan, 1974

Tiegel-Hertfelder 1994
P. Tiegel-Hertfelder, *David Teniers d. J. 1610–1690. Verzeichnis sämtlicher Werke von David Teniers d. J. im Besitz der Staatlichen Museen Kassel. Mit Restaurierungsbericht von P. M. Hilsenbeck-Fritz*, Kassel, 1994

Tietze and Tietze-Conrat 1937/30
Hans Tietze and Erika Tietze-Conrat, *Kritisches Verzeichnis der Werke Albrecht Dürers. Der reife Dürer*, vol. 2, Basle and Leipzig, 1937/38

Tietze-Conrat 1955
E. Tietze-Conrat, *Mantegna: Paintings, Drawings, Engravings*, London, 1955

Udine 1996
Giambattista Tiepolo. Forme e colori. La pittura del Settecento in Friuli, Giuseppe Bergamini (ed.), exh. cat., Chiesa di San Francesco, Udine, 1996

Venice 1969
Dal Ricci al Tiepolo, exh. cat., Palazzo Ducale, Venice, 1969

Venice 1986
Alessandro Bettagno et al., *Bernardo Bellotto. Le vedute di Dresda. Dipinti e incisioni dai musei di Dresda*, exh. cat., Isola di San Giorgio Maggiore, Venice, 1986

Venice 1995
Splendori del Settecento, exh. cat., Ca' Rezzonico, Venice, 1995

Venice 1998
Il mondo di Giacomo Casanova. Un veneziano in Europa 1725–1798, exh. cat., Museo del Settecento Veneziano, Venice, 1998

Venice 2001A
Bernardo Bellotto 1722–1780, Bozena Anna Kowalczyk and Monica da Cortà Fumei (eds), exh. cat., Museo Correr, Venice; *Bernardo Bellotto and the Capitals of Europe*, Edgar Peters Bowron (ed.), exh. cat., Museum of Fine Arts, Houston, 2001

Venice 2001B
Canaletto. Prima Maniera, Alessandro Bettagno and Bozena Anna Kowalczyk (eds), exh. cat., Fondazione Giorgio Cini, Venice, 2001

Vienna 1988
Ecclesia Triumphans Dresdensis, Joachim Menzhausen (ed.), exh. cat., Künstlerhaus Wien, Vienna, 1988

Vienna 2002
Das flämische Stilleben, exh. cat., Palais Harrach, Vienna; Villa Hügel, Essen, 2002

Voss 1924
Hermann Voss, *Die Malerei des Barock in Rom*, Berlin, 1924

Vötsch 2002
Jochen Vötsch, 'Kaiser, Reich und Religion im Spiegel des Kunstkammerinventars von 1595', *Dresdener Kunstblätter*, 46, 2002, no. 6, pp. 208–14

Walford 1991
E. J. Walford, *Jacob van Ruisdael and the Perception of Landscape*, New Haven and London, 1991

Walther 1995
Angelo Walther, *Bernardo Bellotto, genannt Canaletto*, Dresden and Basle, 1995

Warnke 1999
Martin Warnke, *Geschichte der deutschen Kunst. Bd. II: Spätmittelalter und Frühe Neuzeit 1400–1750*, Munich, 1990

Warsaw 1997
Pod Jedna Korona, Królewskie Zbiory Sztuki w Dreznie, exh. cat., Muzeum Narodowe w Warszawie, Warsaw; Staatliche Kunstsammlungen Dresden, 1997

Washington 1978
The Splendor of Dresden. Five Centuries of Art Collecting, exh. cat., National Gallery of Art, Washington DC; Metropolitan Museum of Art, New York; The Fine Arts Museums of San Francisco, 1978–79

Watenabe-O'Kelly 2002
Helen Watenabe-O'Kelly, *Court Culture in Dresden. From Renaissance to Baroque*, Basingstoke and New York, 2002

Weber 1991
Gregor J. M. Weber, *Der Lobtopos des 'lebenden' Bildes. Jan Vos und sein 'Zeege der Schilderkunst' von 1654*, Hildesheim, Zurich and New York, 1991

Weber 1994
Gregor J. M. Weber, 'Italienische Kunsteinkäufer im Dienst der Dresdener Galerie', *Dresdener Hefte*, 40, 1994, pp. 32–42

Weber 1995
Gregor J. M. Weber, 'Ein Gemälde Leonardos für Dresden? Der Ankauf eines Madonnenbildes von Lorenzo di Credi im Jahr 1860', *Dresdener Kunstblätter*, 6, 1995, pp. 166–72

Weber 1996
Gregor J. M. Weber, 'Die Auftragsarbeiten Giovanni Battista Tiepolos für König August III', *Dresdener Kunstblätter*, 40, 1996, pp. 181–90

Weber 1998A
Gregor J. M. Weber, 'Bernardo Bellotto, Nicolaes Berchem und das pastorale Pirna', *Dresdener Kunstblätter*, 42, 1998, pp. 46–53

Weber 1998B
Gregor J. M. Weber, 'Augen der Entrückung', in Weber and Henning 1998, pp. 5–16

Weber and Henning 1998
Gregor J. M. Weber and Andreas Henning, *Der himmelnde Blick. Zur Geschichte eines Bildmotivs von Raffael bis Rotari*, exh. cat., Gemäldegalerie Alte Meister, Dresden, 1998

Weber 1999A
Gregor J. M. Weber, *Pietro Graf Rotari in Dresden. Ein italienischer Maler am Hof König Augusts III. Bestandskatalog*, Dresden, 1999

Weber 1999B
Gregor J. M. Weber, 'The Gallery as Work of Art. The Installation of the Italian Paintings in 1754', in Columbus 1999, pp. 183–97

Weber 2000A
Gregor J. M. Weber, 'Bellotto's verbeterde werkelijkheid', *Kunstschrift*, 44, 2000, no. 4, pp. 18–27

Weber 2000B
Gregor J. M. Weber, 'Ein Ehrenplatz in Dresden. "Die Heilige Nacht" Correggios 1746–1816', in Dresden 2000B, pp. 45–58

Weimar 2002
Rolf Bothe and Ulrich Haussmann, *Goethes 'Bildergalerie'. Die Anfänge der Kunstsammlungen zu Weimar*, exh. cat., Kunstsammlungen zu Weimar, 2002

Weinart 1777
Benjamin Gottfried Weinart, *Topographische Geschichte der Stadt Dresden und der um dieselbe herum liegenden Gegenden*, Dresden, 1777 (reprint Leipzig, 1976)

Weizsäcker 1900
Heinrich Weizsäcker, *Catalog der Gemälde-Gallerie des Städelschen Kunstinstituts in Frankfurt am Main. Erste Abteilung. Die Werke der älteren Meister vom 14. bis zum 18. Jahrhundert*, Frankfurt am Main, 1900

Wethey 1969
Harold E. Wethey, *The Paintings of Titian. Volume I: The Religious Paintings*, London, 1969

Wethey 1971
Harold E. Wethey, *The Paintings of Titian. Volume II: The Portraits*, London, 1971

Wild 1980
Doris Wild, *Nicolas Poussin*, 2 vols, Zurich, 1980

Winckelmann 1764
Johann Joachim Winckelmann, *Geschichte der Kunst des Altertums*, Dresden, 1764

Winckelmann 1925
Johann Joachim Winckelmann, *Kleine Schriften und Briefe*, H. Uhde-Bernays (ed.), Leipzig, 1925

Winckelmann/Rehm 1968
Johann Joachim Winckelmann, 'Gedancken über die Nachahmung der Griechischen Werke in der Mahlerey and Bildhauerkunst', in *Winckelmann, Kleine Schriften, Vorreden, Entwürfe*, Walther Rehm (ed.), Berlin, 1968

Winkler 1964
Friedrich Winkler, *Das Werk von Hugo van der Goes*, Berlin, 1964

Winkler 1989
Der Verkauf an Dresden. Dresden und Modena, aus der Geschichte zweier Galerien, Johannes Winkler (ed.), Modena, 1989

Woermann 1884/85
Karl Woermann, 'Dürer's männliches Bildniss von 1521 in der Dresdner Galerie', in *Repertorium für Kunstwissenschaft*, 7, 1884, pp. 446–49; 8, 1885, pp. 436–38

Woermann 1887
Karl Woermann, *Katalog der Königlichen Gemäldegalerie zu Dresden*, Dresden, 1887 (7th edition, 1908)

Woermann 1894
Karl Woermann, 'Ismael et Anton Raphael Mengs', *Zeitschrift für bildende Kunst*, Neue Serie V, 1894, p. 170

Woermann 1924
Karl Woermann, *Lebenserinnerungen eines Achtzigjährigen*, Leipzig, 1924

Wright 1984
Christopher Wright, *Poussin Paintings. A Catalogue Raisonné*, London, 1984

Zanotti 1739
Giampietro Zanotti, *Storia dell'Accademia Clementina*, 2 vols, Bologna, 1739

Zimmermann 1912
E. Heinrich Zimmermann, *Watteau*, Stuttgart and Leipzig, 1912

Zimmermann 1987
Horst Zimmermann, 'Zur Erwerbungsgeschichte der Gemäldegalerie Neue Meister', in *Gemäldegalerie Dresden, Neue Meister, 19. and 20. Jahrhundert. Bestandskatalog*, Staatliche Kunstsammlungen Dresden, 1987, pp. 9–53

Zurich 1971
Kunstschätze aus Dresden, Zurich, 1971